LOFOTEN ISLAND

TRAVEL GUIDE 2024

Arctic Wonders Unlocked: Your Manual
to Norway's Top Attractions, Culture,
Hidden Gems,and coastal adventures

RICK CAGE

Table of Content

Introduction

An Overview of the Island of Lofoten

The Lofoten Islands are an awe-inspiring archipelago that can be found off the northwest coast of Norway. These islands are famous for their breathtaking scenery and attractive fishing settlements.

Geographically speaking, the islands are situated inside the Arctic Circle, and they are characterized by their majestic mountains, deep fjords, and untouched beaches. There are several notable peaks, such as the well-known Olstind and the terrifying cliffs of the Troll Wall.

Despite its high latitude, Lofoten has a climate that is more temperate than other regions that are located at comparable latitudes. This is because the Gulf Stream is responsible for the milder temperature that Lofoten enjoys. During the summer, there are more daylight hours than during the winter, which is rather peaceful.

The islands have a strong maritime tradition, with red-painted fishing cottages known as "rorbuer" dotting the shoreline. Because the islands have historically been renowned for fishing, they have a rich maritime legacy.
-Over many centuries, cod fishing has been a historic activity.

- **Outdoor Activities:-** A sanctuary for outdoor lovers, Lofoten provides outstanding chances for hiking, climbing, and skiing. The islands are particularly famous for kayaking, fishing expeditions, and animal watching.
- **Northern Lights: -** Thanks to its high latitude, Lofoten affords a wonderful opportunity to experience the Northern Lights throughout the winter months.
- **Villages and Culture: -** Quaint fishing villages like Reine and Henningsvær display traditional architecture and a close-knit community. - The culture

is heavily entrenched in fishing traditions, with a combination of contemporary art and activities.

- **Accessibility:** - Accessible by boat or air, Lofoten's remoteness adds to its charm. The drive itself gives spectacular views of the surrounding countryside.

In essence, the Lofoten Islands fascinate tourists with a perfect combination of natural beauty, outdoor experiences, and a rich cultural tapestry built by centuries of marine history.

Brief History

Norway's Lofoten attracts visitors from all over the globe, but it also has a rich history. From the Viking Age through to the creation of Norway's rich fishing and seafood industries, this is the narrative of Lofoten.

The Lofoten islands in Northern Norway are renowned today as a famous tourist destination. Their natural beauty draws hikers, photographers, and even surfers to the north. However, Lofoten possesses a wealth of historical significance as well.

Evidence of human activity is estimated to date back at least 11,000 years. People have been calling the islands home for nearly as long as anyplace else in Northern Europe. Come with me as I explore the reasons behind this.

Until the 1960s, Norway's major industry was cod. In many respects, the history of Norway is the history of cod fishing. And nowhere in Norway is more vital to cod fishing than the Lofoten Islands.

Lofoten in the Viking Age

There's evidence that people existed in Lofoten before the Viking Age. Archaeological findings from the late stone period, about 5,500 years ago, provide significant traces. There's also some evidence going back earlier than that. But the key data, that we can create a picture from, comes from the Viking Age itself.

The town of Vågan is the earliest known town founded in all of Northern Norway. It was situated on the southern edge of East Lofoten and is adjacent to the current settlement of Kabelvåg, not far from Svolvær.

Many of the archaeological artifacts we have, from the Iron Age and Viking Age, may be discovered further west near Borg on Vestvågøy.

During the Viking Age, chieftains were governed by a blend of alliances and might. Strategic marriages and soft power — giving presents and holding feasts – were as vital as waging wars and killing foes. Consider this: it's more advantageous to keep individuals alive as long as they serve your interests.

One chieftain we know of from Borg was the formidable Oláfr. As well as being known as Uni-brow, he was also thought to be a hammer; a skin-changer, or werewolf. That alone was probably enough to retain his reputation of power and enabled him to dominate over the lush fields in the east of Vestvågøy.

In his tomb, we uncover, among other things, gold-leafed glassware from overseas. This would have been highly exceptional and set Oláfr out as a well-connected and powerful guy.

King Olav and Lofoten

Also renowned in the history of the region was Thorir the Stag (Þórir Hjort) from Austvågøy. He was recognized chiefly as an opponent of King Olav Tryggvason, who unified Norway and launched the Christianisation of the kingdom.

Olav was a brutal conqueror of territories and many chiefs converted without violence, hesitant to oppose the King in combat.

Thorir, however, was a passionate opponent of the king and determined to stand up to what he viewed as oppression. A deadly conflict erupted with enormous casualties on both sides. Eventually, the King was successful, but it was a critical event in their history.

In most stories, the King slew Thorir personally by hurling a spear at him. Some claim that as his corpse dropped to the ground a stag sprang out and raced into the forest.

Vågan would soon become the power core for the area and the local assembly (Thing or Þing) was convened there. King Olav and his successors would soon start to gain a considerable amount of money from the region owing to Lofoten's most beneficial resource: Cod.

There's something in the air

If you arrive in Lofoten in early summer, you'll start to smell the unmistakable fragrance of fish in the air. It's not merely the fragrance of fishing communities but something stronger. The cause for this is tørrfisk or stockfish.

Having a tremendous lot of fish, and being virtually at the top of the globe, is not all that beneficial. You can sell locally and maybe sell to the full business without your fish turning bad.There are techniques for preserving the meat, of course, salting, smoking, and icing for example, but they may be pricey.

Lofoten, however, has some benefits when it comes to cod. In this instance, it's the strong marine winds coming off the Norwegian Sea.

Residents noticed that by hanging the fish in the breeze, the flesh would dry and then could be preserved and carried virtually forever, at no further expense! Once soaked in water, the meat is rehydrated and becomes virtually as good as new.

This is an extraordinary way of preserving food that is unique to Lofoten. Many other sites have tried but the air is either too damp or too dry and the temperature is either too hot or too chilly.

Sales of Norwegian stockfish—the term given to dried cod—around the globe were considerable and the great majority came from Lofoten. Trade in Lofoten stockfish remains on to this day and you can obtain supply in most places around the globe.

Location, location, location

Lofoten is not only wonderful for fishing because it's on the shore. There's a natural advantage. Through much of Northern Norway, the seas are quite cold. This is fantastic for breeding string healthy fish but it's not so great for spawning. The freezing waters are too harsh for young fish to survive, therefore the fish need to go south to reproduce.

Lofoten, however, is surrounded by comparatively gentle water. The impact of the Gulf Stream, North Atlantic Current, and Norwegian Current combines to make the temperature and seas in the region significantly warmer than they would otherwise be.

The region is, in fact, home to the greatest anomaly in temperature relative to latitude anywhere in the globe.

All of this implies that Lofoten offers the optimal spawning circumstances for Arctic cod. Every winter, cod throng the oceans in their hundreds, giving lucrative pickings for fishermen.

Lofoten is so great for cod fishing that fishermen would travel from all over the globe to help get as much of the fish landed as possible to guarantee worldwide supplies were maintained.

This led to the creation of the rorbu - modest cottages designed to lodge the visiting fisherman. These began in the year 1120 when King Øistein ordered them to be erected. These were two-room huts, frequently on stilts, directly near the water.

The word rorbu translates as 'small cottage for persons who row' and they may still be found in Lofoten today. Nowadays they're not so much cabins to house itinerant fishermen but modest – and oftentimes expensive – housing for the Island's visitors.

Lofoten in Norse Mythology

Known as Ketils Saga Hoengs, the Saga of Ketill Trout is one of the Icelandic legendary sagas. These are the legends of ancient Scandinavia before Iceland existed, that offer us much of our knowledge of early Norse folklore, history, and traditions.

From Hrafnista came a guy named Ketill, son of Hallbjörn Half-troll. His father, as the name implies, was a powerful, mighty, and courageous guy who was admired by everybody. Ketill, however, was the reverse of his father. He was calm and he lacked the spirit of adventure commonly conferred to heroes in legend!

When things got hard, and Ketill was a teenager, he grew weary of having no food and resolved to do something about it. Borrowing his family's boat he slipped out in the night and rowed North

He discovered magnificent fishing fields and loaded his boat with plentiful fish. As he beached his boat for the night, he saw a hole filled with the flesh and bones of people and other creatures. Ketill has unintentionally stumbled on an island of cannibal trolls!

He was unable to make his getaway without meeting Surtr the Black and Kaldrann the Cold Moustache. Ketill managed to hold them off long enough to escape and he came home triumphant, with a ship full of fish and a fine story to tell.

That wasn't Ketill's only experience, however. A few years later the hunger came and so this time Ketill rowed even farther, all the way up to Lofoten, where he loaded his ship with the copious fish. On the island of Skrova in East Lofoten he meets two troll ladies who warn him that the Tröllaþing - a gathering of trolls – is taking place that night.

Ketill watched the most terrible and massive of trolls assembling on the island. He possessed magical abilities and sorcery unlike anything witnessed by humans before.Fearing for his life he concealed himself behind a thick cover of branches and leaves and kept himself awake to avoid handing himself up to the trolls.

Once again, Ketill came home a hero and that was his final excursion to Lofoten.

The Italian cod

If you thought Lofoten is isolated then Røst, some 10km away from the rest of Lofoten and 100km away from the mainland establishes new levels of isolation!

Like Lofoten, the region of Røst – comprising 350 islets and skerries in total including the main island, Røstlandet – is largely concentrated upon fishing and, in winter, the population grows by 3 or 4 times.

We don't always know the precise narrative of how trade routes come up. Many of them date back to the periods when people were habitually keeping note of their history.

In 1432 the Venetian sea-captain Pietro Querini was shipwrecked and was saved by the islanders of Røstlandet. Out of 68 crew, just 11 survived, being recovered a month after they were first shipwrecked. They remained in the region for three months before returning to Venice.

After returning home Querini presented an excellent depiction of the medieval lives of the people there. He explained how they survived by collecting and drying fish and how the inhabitants were religious and pleasant.

Querini took some of the excellent and adaptable Stockfish and also popularised it in the Venice region. It is still served there today and is called Baccalà all vincentina. And that's how a chance 15th-century shipwreck gave birth to a worldwide commerce route in Stockfish and a distinctive dish that exists to this day!

Chapter 1

Getting To The Lofoten Island

Transportation choices

Lofoten is a dream vacation for many people all over the globe. Here are all your travel choices for going to these isolated islands in Northern Norway.

The spectacular natural splendor of Norway's Lofoten islands lures people from around the globe. Dramatic mountains rising out of the water deliver an amazing greeting, but it's the lovely towns, sandy beaches, and vistas from the infinite hiking paths that will linger in your mind for years to come.

Many travelers arrange an itinerary centered on the features of the Lofoten Islands such as certain hiking paths or places to stay. But preparing how to travel to this isolated corner of Northern Norway is just as vital.

Picking the best travel choice will help you make the most of your stay on the islands. It might also help the travel itself become part of your holiday.

Simply stated, you either pay with money or with time. Flying there is pricey but easy, while the cheaper choices require doing battle with boat timings and rental car agencies.

So, first things first, there is not one "best way" to arrive at Lofoten. The optimal way for you relies on your travel preferences, but also on your target destination and planned schedule once you arrive.

For example, if you are going to utilize Svolvaer as a base and take day excursions out to the western islands, you should look at choices that bring you to Svolvær.

If you are more interested in trekking and visiting distant beaches, it would be best for you to come near the western end of the archipelago.

In addition, consider if you will be driving and how it can affect your choice of trip. Now, let's look at the primary alternatives in more detail

Flying to Lofoten

There are a few small airports in Lofoten but they are modest compared to airports on the mainland with short runways.

Both Leknes (LKN) and Svolvær (SVJ) are normally serviced by Widerøe propellor aircraft flying from Bodø.

This implies that traveling to Lofoten normally necessitates a trip to Bodø first, or at least transit to Bodø by other means. During the summer season, Widerøe normally provides direct flights from Oslo to Svolvær.

Another alternative is to travel to Harstad/Narvik airport, popularly known as Evenes. While not on the islands, the airport's longer runway means it is serviced by bigger flights from Oslo. From Evenes, there is a direct (although irregular) bus service to Svolvær.

Renting a vehicle from Evenes (and the other airports) is also available. If you are traveling to Lofoten proper, take in mind that rental vehicle availability on the islands is relatively restricted, particularly in the summer.

Book a vehicle in advance. If you arrive without a vehicle in the peak season, chances are you will not locate one. The rental vehicle offices may not even be open if they have received no reservations. You may check rental costs in Svolvær here.

Because traveling to the islands is pricey, many people opt to go by plane to Bodø instead. From Bodø, there is a variety of ferries that go across to Lofoten including a vehicle ferry to Moskenes.

Driving to Lofoten

Most individuals going to Lofoten without their automobile opt to fly to Bodø and hire a car in Bodø.

While a lengthier road trip throughout Norway is a desire of many, you'll practically need two days simply to go up to Bodø from Oslo, and that's without including any sightseeing.

From Bodø, the best alternative for driving is the daily car ferry to Moskenes at the western extremity of the archipelago. It takes slightly over three hours.

It's also feasible to drive without utilizing the car ferry. However, traveling from Bodø to Moskenes takes up to 8 hours and that still involves a smaller automobile ferry crossing from Bognes to Lodingen.

Driving an entirely ferry-free route via Narvik takes at least 8.5 hours. Knock off around two hours if you're going to Svolvær.

Travel to Lofoten via public transport

Given the busy highways during the summer, more individuals are preferring to get to Lofoten via public transit

It's doable, as long as you have some patience. From Oslo, you may travel by rail to Bodø. However, the Oslo to Trondheim train takes roughly seven hours, followed by up to 10 hours on the Trondheim to Bodø train.

Night trains operate on both lines thus it's feasible to travel by rail between Oslo and Bodø within 24 hours. However, there are no showers on Norwegian trains, so you may opt to stay a night in Trondheim to break up the ride.

There is also the opportunity to take a shower at a neighboring hotel upon arrival for an additional price. You'll find out more about this choice on the train.

Ferries to Lofoten

From Bodø, there are three ways to reach Lofoten. Firstly, it's feasible to board the Moskenes automobile ferry as a foot passenger. A smaller passenger-only express boat links Bodø and Svolvær.

It takes slightly over three hours with multiple stops at islands and small settlements along the route.

Finally, you may join the Norwegian coastal cruise as a port-to-port passenger between Bodø and Stamsund or Svolvær.

While longer (the complete journey from Bodø to Svolvær takes six hours) and more costly, the Hurtigruten doubles as a tourist cruise along the mountainous Lofoten coastline between Stamsund and Svolvær.

If you wish, you may go all the way from Bergen, Ålesund, or Trondheim on the Hurtigruten or Havila ships.

Coastal ships leave Bergen at 8.30 pm most days and arrive in Svolvær around 72 hours later.

However, you're unlikely to find a rate for the three-night journey for under $800 per person, although that would normally include a stateroom and meals.

Here are some recommendations for traveling to and around Lofoten:

- **By Plane:** The closest airport to Lofoten is Harstad/Narvik Airport, which is approximately a 2-hour drive from Svolvær, the main town in Lofoten.

From the airport, you may hire a vehicle, take a cab, or utilize public transit to travel to Lofoten.

- **By car:** Lofoten is linked to the mainland by various bridges and tunnels, so it's possible to travel there from different regions of Norway. However, be warned that parts of the roads in Lofoten are small and twisty, so driving may be tough, particularly in winter.

- **By bus:** Various bus companies provide services to and from Lofoten, including Nordlandsekspressen and Arctic Route. Buses are a decent choice if you don't want to drive yourself, but be aware that services may be restricted outside of high season.

- **By ferry:** Various ferry lines link Lofoten to other regions of Norway, including Bodø, Moskenes, and Skutvik. Ferries are a lovely method to get to Lofoten and may also be utilized to go about the archipelago.

- **By bike:** Lofoten is a popular location for cycling, and there are various rental shops where you may hire bikes. However, be warned that the terrain may be tough, with steep slopes and tight roads.

- **By foot**: Lofoten is a hiker's heaven, with several gorgeous paths that highlight the archipelago's rough nature. Be careful to bring sturdy shoes and warm clothes, since the weather may be unpredictable.

- **Hitchhiking:** Hitchhiking is reasonably popular and regarded as safe in Lofoten. Locals and tourists regularly provide rides, particularly in the warmer months.

Once you're in Lofoten, there are various choices for moving about. Rental vehicles are available at the airport and in various cities, however, be advised that parking might be restricted in some locations. Buses are a decent alternative for lengthier excursions, and various taxi companies operate in the area. Additionally, many sites and towns in Lofoten are within riding distance, so hiring a bike may be a fun and eco-friendly way to get about.

Airports in Lofoten Islands

The principal access to the Lofoten Islands is by plane travel. The primary airport servicing the area is:

Leknes Airport (LKN):

Located on the island of Vestvågøya, Leknes Airport is strategically positioned in the archipelago.

It provides domestic flights linking Lofoten to major Norwegian towns such as Oslo and Bodø.

For those considering other routes, you may also fly into airports on the mainland and then utilize other transit alternatives to reach Lofoten. Some airports on the mainland with strong connections include:

Bodø Airport (BOO):

Located on the mainland, Bodø Airport is a typical starting point for visitors heading to Lofoten.

Regular flights link Bodø to numerous Norwegian cities.

Harstad/Narvik Airport (EVE):

Situated on the mainland, this airport serves the broader area and provides flights to and from Oslo.

Upon landing at these airports, passengers may then take a mix of ferries, buses, or rental automobiles to reach the Lofoten Islands, allowing a chance to experience the magnificent route to the archipelago.

Weather and Best Time to Visit

Planning on visiting the Lofoten Islands in northern Norway, but have no clue when to go?

Well, the good news is that Lofoten is a fantastic experience in all weather and all seasons, so you can't select the incorrect time. Deciding when the ideal time to visit the Lofoten Islands depends on what sort of experience you desire for yourself and what aspects you value the most while traveling. Such as crowds, money, travel style, what natural experiences you like, and other personal preferences.

The bad news? Deciding when to visit the Lofoten Islands may be challenging, particularly if you're an "I want to experience it all at once" sort of tourist since every season has its apparent merits and drawbacks. For instance, is difficult to enjoy both northern lights and the midnight sun in one Lofoten trip. (But it just means you have the ideal reason to go back, right?).

Hopefully, I can help make your selection at least a little bit simpler by separating the advantages and negatives below - season by season!

Summer In Lofoten (June – August)

Why Summer In Lofoten Is Amazing

The most popular season to visit Lofoten is probably during summer. The summer months are the peak season in this region of the country, and Lofoten is a favorite summer destination among both domestic and foreign tourists, especially between mid-June and mid-August. This is the season of the year when the weather conditions are typically on their best behavior, which is excellent for hanging out at one of the fantastic beaches, camping, hiking, fishing, and other outdoor activities in Lofoten.

The nicest part about coming in summer is the magnificent and bucket-list-worthy midnight sun! Between May 26 and July 17, you receive 24 hours of daylight in Lofoten, which provides you more time to appreciate the great environment without ever having a headlamp. I promise nothing can genuinely compare with going up a mountain in Lofoten in the midnight sun. After July 17 it becomes steadily darker until autumn, so late July and August are still ideal dates to visit if you desire those longer days on your journey to the north.

There are usually a lot of activities going on in Lofoten during peak season, and pretty much every single restaurant, hotel, museum, excursion, and attraction will be accessible throughout the summer months. (Which regrettably is not the case for the previous three seasons – but more on that later on).

The Downside Of Summer In Lofoten

The greatest negative of visiting Lofoten in summer? The large crowds. Now, this isn't always a problem - it all depends on what type of vacation you're planning for yourself. Just make sure you're prepared for lengthier waits and put in additional time for things you want to undertake. High season also implies higher rates for hotels and vehicle rentals so remember to book early if you can. Not only will it be simpler on your money, but you can also risk ending yourself with no bed to sleep in and no vehicle to drive if you snooze. Also, warn that you won't be able to observe northern lights during summer in Lofoten.

Fall In Lofoten (August – October)

Why Fall In Lofoten Is Amazing

Fall in northern Norway is a very brief occurrence that spans from around late August until the beginning or middle of October. By visiting Lofoten during autumn you'll get to see the magnificent archipelago with fewer tourists than in summer, which for many visitors is a comfort compared to visiting Lofoten in the middle of July (myself included). If you're fortunate you may get to witness the fantastic clear autumn weather we occasionally get up here, and mixed with the magnificent fall colors Lofoten is quite the sight.

If you're very fortunate, you may even get to witness the northern lights! The odds of viewing northern lights in Lofoten are fairly excellent in late September and October. If is vital for you to witness the midnight sun, however, you should visit Lofoten before September since the midnight sun formally departs Lofoten on July 17th. The evenings are still relatively long in the weeks following, however, which generates the most beautiful light conditions and sunsets around autumn.

You may also discover that both flights, lodging, and vehicle hire are a bit cheaper than in the summer months, which is ideal if you're on a tight budget.

The Downside Of Fall In Lofoten

Since October qualifies as low season in Lofoten you should bear in mind that certain restaurants, museums, excursions, and other attractions may be unavailable. So explore all of the must-do activities on your agenda before arranging a vacation to Lofoten in autumn.

You should also know that your chances of receiving severe weather during your Lofoten vacation are greater in autumn compared to the summer months, and if you're unfortunate it might rain a lot, particularly in late September and October. You could even get to experience a truly arctic autumn storm, which is a lot more comfy than it sounds (unless you're on a boat, then really hurts). If it occurs, simply put on some wool socks, prepare some hot chocolate, and drink it by the fireplace (if you have one) in your rorbu and listen to the storm outside.. pure Norway pleasure.

Winter In Lofoten (November – March)

Why Winter In Lofoten Is Amazing

Visiting Lofoten during winter is an unusual, although wonderful experience. Between November and March – sometimes longer – you get to experience the stunning sight of snow-covered trees and mountain peaks while touring the lovely fishermen commfishermen'sofoten has to offer. Since trekking isn't an option (without snowshoes) you should spend your days cross-country skiing or ice fishing instead, and your evenings searching for northern lights. Sounds amazing, right? It is!

And do you know what the absolute greatest thing about winter in Lofoten is? The absence of crowds! If you appreciate an off-the-beaten-path style of travel, or simply sincerely despise other human people, you should visit Lofoten in the winter. And while it seems very frigid, Lofoten has a coastal climate which means it doesn't get that cold. And as a bonus - you'll discover that flights, hotel, vehicle hire, and tours/activities are substantially cheaper than during peak season.

Visiting Lofoten in winter is also fantastic for individuals who enjoy ski touring since there are a wide variety of stunning mountains to tackle. Inexperienced persons should however never go on such an activity without sufficient training and a guide. Avalanches are not rare up here owing to our mild winters.

The Downsides Of Winter In Lofoten

I'm not going to lie, it gets gloomy up here during winter, particularly between December and February. But that's not always a bad thing as long as you make use of the few hours of daylight you have each day. Heck, I even hear some tourists find it exotic! Those gloomy days are excellent for bonfires on the coast or cuddling up in front of the fireplace in a rorbu.

Beware that certain restaurants and sites may be closed since it is off-season.. I also strongly suggest avoiding visiting Lofoten, or rural Norway in general, around Christmas or Easter. Norwegians take their holidays seriously and during these holidays you'll come to learn that pretty much everything is closed. You'll scarcely see anybody since everyone will be at home with their family eating pinnekjøtt, ribbe, or lutefisk and drinking gløgg or aquavit till their trousers rupture due to excessive pressure.

If you're planning on driving your way across Lofoten, I know that some of you will be anxious about driving in this region of Norway in winter. I will agree it may be tough at times, much more so if you're not accustomed to winter driving in general, but if you're attentive and take measures you should be just fine!

Spring In Lofoten (March-May)

Why Spring In Lofoten Is Amazing

Visiting in spring is a beautiful chance to explore Lofoten with more daylight than in the winter months, but without the massive flow of visitors one may anticipate in summer. This is perfect for those of you who want to avoid crowds or those who want to save some money on traveling in the low season without sacrificing the sunshine.

In March and April, you may view northern lights if you're fortunate, before the wonderful midnight sun season comes in May. Hiking without snowshoes or skis may be feasible in spring if the weather and snow conditions allow it. Many summits will be covered in snow until July, however, and avalanches are not unusual - so do study or consult an experienced local before venturing out on a walk.

The Downsides Of Spring In Lofoten

Keep in mind that the weather in Lofoten is quite unpredictable in Spring, and the temperatures fluctuate each year. In our region of the nation, it may go from one meter of snow (or wet snow that damages all of your lovely shoes) to immediate "summer" temps within the period of a few days in Spring. And the worst thing is that this procedure might happen in March or it can happen in late June, there is no way of knowing. Check the weather before you leave and prepare appropriately. Also, bear in mind that they can change frequently, so don't become too discouraged if it forecasts a lot of rain or snow. And remember that because Spring is before peak season in Lofoten, there can be restaurants and attractions that haven't opened yet.

My Opinion: The Best Time To Visit Lofoten Islands

That was a lot of information and a lot of pros and negatives, right? Now, to sum it all up for you I considered the perfect time to visit Lofoten Islands. Based on my own experience visiting Lofoten multiple times.

Lofoten In September

My favorite season in northern Norway in general is autumn. In late August or September, your odds of clear weather are fair without the crowds being overwhelming. The evenings are still brighter despite the midnight sun being gone, which is excellent for trekking. Incredible lighting conditions, magnificent autumn colors, and decent chances of northern lights. Can be cheaper than during the busy season.

Lofoten In June

If you visit Lofoten in early June you'll have the upsides of the summer season without the enormous crowds, like seeing the midnight sun. Decent likelihood of nice weather, but it may still be chilly, particularly at night, so pack thermals and heavy layers if you intend to spend some time outside. Can be cheaper than during the busy season.

Lofoten In March Or April

Winter in Lofoten may be a magnificent experience. Visit in March or April for the greatest possibilities of experiencing the snow-covered countryside with a clear sky. You also have more daylight than between December and February, and the probability of witnessing northern lights is good. Will be a lot cheaper than during the busy season.

Clothes and Accessories to carry for your Travel

When preparing for your vacation to the Lofoten Islands, consider the changing weather and outdoor activities. Here's a proposed list of outfits and accessories:

Layered Clothing:
- Thermal base layers for warmth.
- Insulating layers like fleece or down coats.
- Waterproof and windproof outer layers.

Waterproof Gear:
- Waterproof jacket with a hood.
- Waterproof trousers for outdoor activities.

Warm Accessories:
- Hat, gloves, and a scarf for cooler climates.
- Warm socks and strong, waterproof footwear for trekking.

Outdoor Apparel:
- Comfortable hiking pants or leggings.
- Long-sleeved shirts for sun protection and warmth.

Swimwear:

- If you intend on having a plunge in the Arctic seas or enjoying a sauna.

Accessories:

Backpack:

- A daypack for transporting necessities during outdoor activities.

Sun Protection:

- Sunglasses with UV protection.
- Sunscreen with a high SPF.

Electronics:

- Camera for photographing the gorgeous scenery.
- Portable charger for electrical gadgets.

Navigation:

- Map and compass or GPS for trekking activities.

Water Bottle:

- Stay hydrated with a reusable water bottle.

Travel Adapters:

- European-style power adapters for charging electronics.

First Aid Kit:

- Basic first aid items for emergencies.

Insect Repellent:

- Depending on the season, particularly if you want to visit nature paths.

Remember to check the weather prediction before your travel and alter your packing list appropriately. Lofoten's weather may be unpredictable, so having varied clothing choices will guarantee you're prepared for any scenario.

Chapter 2

Accomodation Options (Where to stay in the Lofoten Island)

Visiting the Lofoten Islands in Norway is a dream: the archipelago is such a unique area that it's well worth the money and the time required to journey here. If you're planning a vacation to the Lofoten Islands and you're ready to choose where to stay in the Lofoten Islands, you undoubtedly have plenty of possibilities.

From roubers (ancient fishing cottages turned into flats) to hotels, hostels, and even campgrounds, you will be spoilt with options to the point where selecting a spot may seem overwhelming.

Where To Stay In The Lofoten Islands

There are a handful of factors you need to consider when deciding where to stay in the Lofoten Islands.

It's a vast archipelago, and it takes a few hours to drive from one side to the other: it is completely conceivable, but we urge you to take your time to drive, stop, explore, drive again, walk, dine, and overall enjoy the region.

The second item you may need to consider is accessibility: the most major towns are Svolvaer and Leknes and offer a fantastic range of eating places and things to do. The tiniest villages are obviously more lovely and scenic, but the eating options are restricted, and you need to compromise and finally spend more to acquire meals.

We did go for both options: Svolvaer and also a few little places. From a gastronomic viewpoint, we didn't even contemplate staying or eating in Leknes since the variety of restaurants is constrained.

Anker Brygge – Svolvaer

in town = £382.00 incl B/fast (can get cheaper)

Anker Brygge might be your first approach to the Lofoten Islands, and you'll be shocked by how magnificent this location is. It provides accommodations in traditional Norwegian fishermen's huts, all with free WiFi and sea or quay views. Breakfast is nothing remarkable, but the coffee is decent.

Top tip: reserve a supper at Kjøkkenet, the on-site restaurant, and opt for the "grandma's menu" to experience the traditional dishes from the Lofoten Islands, largely based on stockfish and cod. It's a touch pricy, but it's a beautiful spot to dine, and it's entirely worth it. For a fast and less costly lunch/dinner, travel to Bacalao where you may enjoy local and foreign cuisine.

Price range: 1,500 to 3,000 NOK per night ($160 – $320 / 145€ – 290€).

Address: Lamholmen 1, 8300 Svolvær, Norway

Lofoten Rorbuhotell – Sørvågen

Located just 5 minutes drive from Reine and 10 minutes from Hamnøy, the two biggest attractions in the Lofoten Islands, Lofoten Rorbuhotell is distinctively Norwegian. The original fishermen's homes have been transformed into individual flats, all equipped with a kitchen, a bathroom, and a balcony. The main building, where the reception and the restaurant are housed, is roughly 1 Km on foot from the Rorbuer and you may drive or walk.

Top tip: Plan a supper at Maren Anna, a pleasant and friendly local restaurant specializing in local fresh items, primarily fish. Drive to the little town of Å and eat a cinnamon bun at

the globally famous The Bakery, operating since 1844 in a classic Trønder and Nordland home (open only in summer!)
Address: Besselvågveien 8, 8392 Sørvågen, Norway

Hattvika Lodge – Ballstad *unavailable.*

Hattvika is perhaps the spot we enjoyed the best during our vacation in the Lofoten Islands. It's distant from the most touristic locations, and it's nice, personal, and wonderful. Heaven on earth is forever searching for a pleasant and attractive setting. You may opt for the largest apartment to share with friends and family or for the smallest one; dormitories are available for huge groups (mid-June to mid-August). We had the largest and most beautiful flat, additionally equipped with a private sauna!. Still, it provides an unparalleled experience to its guests: the chance to visit the only Cod Liver Taste Depot in the World. Kristian, the proprietor of Hattvika, will offer you lots of information on things to do and see, and he will also be ready to arrange daily tours and treks.

Top tip: sample the meals at Himmel & Havn, situated adjacent to Hattvika Lodge, and the pastries at 8373 Cafe, 5 minutes from the Lodge.

Price range: 1,900 to 10,000 NOK per night ($205 – $1080 / 183€ – 970€).

Address: Hattvikveien 14, 8373 Ballstad, Norway

Our ultimate suggestions for accommodation in Lofoten Islands.

If we did it again (and we will!), we would stay at Hattvika Lodge: the view is beautiful, the environment is calm and pleasant, and in total honesty, you can visit every single part of the Lofoten Islands with only a couple of hours driving.

But if your aim is to road-tour around the Lofoten Islands, and you want to optimize your experience, you may simply reserve the three locations we mentioned in this guide. It makes sense to spend a day in Svolvaer and then go down to Sørvågen to see Reine and Hamnøy before moving "center-north" to Ballstad for a few days to tour the region and finally visit again something you've missed

The Lofoten Islands offer various communities that need to be visited, but what I propose is to design your schedule according to the lodgings where you will stay.

I suggest avoiding remaining in one place but moving about throughout your vacation. Perhaps you might select one accommodation in the north, one in a central location, and a third near the southern edge of the Islands.

Here are the Rorbuer I enjoyed during my travels to the Lofoten Islands:

Å Rorbuer

This settlement is quaint: it is situated in Å, the southernmost village of the Lofoten Islands, and is ideally positioned and remote enough to view the northern lights with the naked eye! It was exactly outside this town when I witnessed my first Northern Lights.

So, well, I could only encourage you to stay at Å Rorbuer. You may book your reservation for a one-bedroom rorbu for exquisite moments of peace, or rent a 3-bedroom apartment that can accommodate up to 8 people. Near the town there is a restaurant and a pub, however, the Rorbuer have a kitchen.

Address: Å-veien 45, 8392 Sørvågen, Norway

Å-Hamna Rorbuer

Å-Hamna Rorbuer is also situated in Å, a short distance from the Å Rorbuer.

What I enjoyed about staying in these little cottages in Lofoten was the decor, warm yet functional and contemporary, which made my evenings here absolutely unique.

My Rorbu's kitchen was contemporary and featured all the basics for delicious meals (there was even a dishwasher and oven!).

Address: Å-veien 18, 8392 Sørvågen, Norway

Reine Rorbuer

Reine Rorbuer's location is ideal year-round. In summer, you can easily access Reinebringen from your accommodation, and in winter, you'll appreciate staying in one of the few villages with a daily open café and service station.

The view of the Reinebringen is fantastic, many cottages are fitted with underfloor heating and a kitchenette.

However, if you don't always feel like cooking, know that the Gammelbua restaurant will surprise you with local delights!

Address: Reineveien 165, 8390 Reine, Norway

Dove Alloggiare alle Lofoten: Sakrisøy Rorbuer

In fairness, I have to tell you that Sakrisøy Rorbuer was "my first time" in a rorbuer and a magnificent Northern Lights so okay, you could think I'm a little prejudiced.

But I assure you that after the first crush, I can tell you that these Rorbuer are unique and amazing (to begin with, they are not red!).

The town is located across a single island, joined by two bridges. It is situated a short distance between Reine and Hamnøy, possibly the most photographed place in Lofoten. These villas are great for couples, families, or groups of friends.

There are Rorbuer with 1, 2 or 3 bedrooms, excellent for spending a trip together! These apartments are also supplied with a suitable parking place and are positioned in front of the bus stop, useful if you need to commute by public transport.

The Rorbuer overlook the bluest water you've probably ever seen, and rowboats may be leased for free throughout the summer.

Rostad Retro Rorbuer

Rostad Retro Rorbuer is positioned directly on the other side of Sakrisøy Rorbuer, so you will get a lovely view of Reine and the settlement of Sakrisøy, which can make you never want to leave!

The Rostad Retro Rorbuer is the right choice for individuals seeking a fantasy spot to stay overnight, but accommodation in Lofoten where up to 8 persons may stay at the same time.

Another good element of this construction is the location facing west, which will enable you to enjoy spectacular sunsets!

Address: Olenilsøy, 8390 Reine, Norway

Eliassen Rorbuer

It is one of the most photographed towns of the Lofoten Islands.

It was picked on the cover of the Norway guide, so there must be a reason! Staying in this village during your vacation to Lofoten may mean feeling like you're on a movie set.

But don't overlook the wonderful location of this bit of heaven to grab some fantastic shots of the Northern Lights display.

Address: 8390 Hamnøy, Norway

Nusfjord Arctic Resort

The Nusfjord Arctic Resort is in a somewhat secluded place compared to the major attractions of the Lofoten Islands, but I urge you to stay here if you are searching for contemporary accommodation (albeit not cheap!), tucked in a historic fishing hamlet (Nusfjord), equipped with a lot of spas.

Inside the Rorbuer complex, there is a restaurant and a bakery, which will make your meals truly dive into the tastes of the sea.

Address: 8380 Ramberg, Norway

Lofoten Wild Camping and 16 Top Camping Sites (Including Beaches)

Many people come to Lofoten thinking of wild camping in Lofoten in lovely spots. While certainly, this is still feasible, it's grown difficult in recent years owing to the enormous amount of visitors who travel to Lofoten for that.

The numbers put stress on the sensitive ecosystem that has such a limited growth season. Stepping off the path might lead to years and years of restoration for an area of land.

Sure, one person may not make a difference, but when you consider the number of people tenting on sensitive plants, dumping waste, or being rude, it's clear to understand why there have been limitations set on wild camping Lofoten.

Lofoten is not the location for driving off-road and down side roads to locate someplace to wild camp.

Wild camping like this is forbidden in Lofoten. Stay on highways and park only in locations where you will not be a burden to people, animals, and the environment.

Many parking spaces or gravel locations formerly utilized as unofficial campsites are now tagged with "No camping" signs and may no longer be used for wild camping in Lofoten.

Don't remain there if there is a sign warning you not to, it simply destroys it for potential future tourists to Lofoten.

Furthermore, don't use café restrooms to wash yourself, your clothing, or your boots. When we visited Lofoten we spotted dozens of cafés that had signs warning campers not to do this and it's very simple to see why.

Best Campsite

If you're searching for the greatest locations to camp in Lofoten, our Lofoten travel guide includes all the well-known best wild camping and public campsites in Lofoten

In general, campgrounds in Norway and the Lofoten Islands are not locations where you'll find enormous privately owned campsites with tons of amenities like pools, and entertainment. Camping in Norway is often only a plot of land with a few toilets and (maybe) showers.

Occasionally, there might be a cafe or laundry facilities available, but it's not assured.

In many situations, you'll need to pay extra for the showers and washing machines.

Due to the rise in camping in Lofoten, rates have been rising and most campsites will cost between 100-300 NOK for the night. Prices vary depending on how many people there are, whether you're in a campervan or tent, and whether you require an electric hook-up.

1. Uttakliev Beach

Uttakliev Beach in Lofoten used to provide free camping with a great view of one of the nicest beaches in Lofoten.

Nowadays, you need to pay for it. Recent costs for Uttakliev beach camping are 250 NOK per night for a spot.

Several restrooms are available to campers, hikers, and those simply passing by. There are no showers and a lot of the field is open to sheep grazing so you'll have to select your place carefully to avoid pitching in sheep excrement

However, you do have the chance to wake up to a wonderful view of the sea.

There's also a nice stroll along the historic road which follows the shoreline which stretches from Uttakliev beach to Haukland beach. It's largely flat and perfect for running and walking.

Address: Uttakleivveien 238, 8370 Leknes, Norway

2. Haukland beach

Haukland Beach is near Uttakleiv Beach and provides camping.

There are two parking lots, a smaller one with a beach café in the summer season and bathrooms, and a bigger one that has a height requirement to enter into.

If you're in a motorhome or tall-height van then you won't be able to go over the barrier.

While the space surrounding the beach is wide, there is just a tiny area you're permitted to camp on.

Overnight parking is 160 NOK, It's unclear if there's an extra cost if you're camping, although 160 NOK appears to be the price for camping also.

Walking between Haukland Beach and Uttalkiev Beach is a nice coastline hike.

Address: Uttakleivveien 200, 8370 Leknes, Norway

3. Kvalvika beach

Kvalvika Beach is an exceptionally lovely beach and provides hike-in camping inside Lofoddon National Park.

At Kvalvika beach you're surrounded by azure sea and big mountains.

The Kvalvika beach stroll here leads you along part of the way to the famous Ryten climb, across boardwalks and past lakes and limitless vistas.

It's a great area to camp but it may be quite crowded in the summer months. So, if you're imagining being on the beach where it's just your tent or maybe another couple, that's not going to be the case. It'll still be nice, but it's not exactly secluded camping anymore.

You also need to park your vehicle at the beginning of this trek to camp in Lofoten.

The nearby neighborhood, Fredvang, has grown fairly tight about where you can and can't park and now there is a vast car park space. They offer washrooms at the trailhead and drinking water from a tap.

You may also camp in a campervan in the parking lot.

The cost of camping here varies from 150 - 250 NOK. You must pay in cash or by VIPPS to the person at the entry or by putting the money in an envelope supplied.

Address: øya,, 8387 Moskenes, Norway

4. Lofoten Beach Camp on Skagsanden Beach

Skagsanden Beach is near the scenic village of Nusfjord and is in a magnificent setting. Home to Lofoten Beach Camp, Skagsanden Beach features camping for tents and campervans in Lofoten.

It's the best site for midnight sun camping or witnessing the Northern Lights in Lofoten.

The beach is popular for surfing and Lofoten Beach Camp has put up a magnificent café and restaurant, gives surf instruction and rentals, and offers showers. They also feature an electric hook-up for campervan camping in Lofoten (at an additional fee), as well as grey water and chemical waste disposal and drinking water taps.

You cannot book a spot at Lofoten Beach Camp. They encourage you to come before 6 pm in the summer months (but I'd get there early to guarantee you secure a camping space!). The Lofoten Beach camp pricing is from adults 50 NOK and children 12-18 25 NOK each night.

Address: Kjerkveien 45, 8380 Ramberg, Norway

5. Bunes Beach Lofoten

On Lofoten's North shore lies Bunes Beach which provides white sand, hiking, and camping.

This is one of the toughest spots to get to as you need to take a boat from Reine to Bunes Beach. The boat travels from near the Circle K petrol station in Reine and you must pay to park.

The boat operates twice a day and costs 80 NOK per passenger.

Most tourists to Bunes Beach only arrive for the day so it's just you and a smaller number of campers putting up their tents for the evening. However, Bunes is increasingly busier every year.

Storms in this region may leave areas of the beach very covered with debris. Yet, this implies there's an abundant source of driftwood available for making campfires.

Address: Moskenesøya, 8390 Reine, Norway

6. Myrland Beach

Myrland Beach is a picturesque beach at the end of a quiet, single-track road set inside a tiny village of dwellings.

You get spectacular vistas and, of course, a background of mountains.

Maryland Beach itself has white sand and the water here is turquoise. It nearly looks tropical but you can be sure it won't feel tropical!

Address: Myrlandsveien, 8340 Stamsund, Norway

7. Eggum Camping

The little settlement of Eggum, Lofoten sits barely off the main road. To access the beach proper you need to drive down a private road and pay 40 NOK (dropping into a letterbox) if you intend to camp it'll cost 200 NOK

After driving down this road for a couple of km, you'll reach a parking area where you may stroll down to the beach. The beach here is unusual to many of Lofoten's beaches in that it's rocky and not sandy.

It's still gorgeous however and there's a fantastic (although rocky, narrow and steep in spots) coastal route that stretches around the coastline to Unstad.

Unstad Arctic Surf

Unstad Arctic Surf is another famous site for surfing in Lofoten. A short walk from the beach itself, Unstad Arctic Surf is a spacious café and restaurant with a little store, lodging, a sauna, and surf rentals.

You may also camp on their property (for a price) if you're in a campervan.

Address: 8360 Bøstad, Norway

8. Moskenes Camping

Moskenes campground in Lofoten is the only campsite in Lofoten where you get a view of the whole Lofoten Wall - the range of mountains that make up Lofoten.

At the correct time of year, you may occasionally observe passing killer whales as they make their trek past Lofoten.

This is the closest you'll truly come to Reine camping these days considering the current limits on Reinebringen.

Camping at Moskenes in Lofoten is for tents and campervans and there are showers, toilets, a kitchen, and washing machines..

There's also a garbage disposal system for folks with campervans and mobile homes.

There's also a bar and you're well located for seeing some of the most popular sites for photography in Lofoten and the greatest trekking in Lofoten.

Address: Birger Eriksens vei 30, 8392 Sørvågen, Norway

9. Hammerstad Camping

Hammerstad campground is located in the northern section of Lofoten and this campsite in Lofoten includes room for campervans, tents, and mobile homes and has a few sites with electric hook-ups too.

You may also hire boards to explore the fjords from Hammerstad.

Tent camping costs 255 NOK for two persons and one medium-sized tent while campervan camping begins at roughly 300 NOK per night.

Address: Austnesfjordveien 720, 8300 Svolvær, Norway

10. Skårungen camping

Skårungen campground in Svolvaer features a beach bar, sauna and spa, and a beautiful café and restaurant on-site.

There's a shower block and a cooking space accessible for campers as well.

Camping here costs 350-450 NOK.

Address: Ørsvågveien 40, 8310 Kabelvåg, Norway.

11.Brustranda Fjordcamping

Brustranda is located at the end of Rolvsfjord and you get wonderful views from this camping place.

There's a small gift shop and restaurant on site as well as washrooms and showers.

Prices for tent camping start at 250 NOK and it's an extra 10 NOK for usage of the showers.

This is one of the few sites for camping in Lofoten that you can arrange in advance

Address: Valbergsveien 851, 8370 Leknes, Norway

12.   Lofoten Camping Storfjord

With a woodfired hot tub and sauna for hire and a spacious space for tents and campervans near a lake, Lofoten Camp Storfjord is one of the finest locations to camp in Lofoten.

Tents cost from 300 NOK per night, and 350 NOK per night for motorhomes.

Address: Hagskarveien 336, 8340 Stamsund, Norway

13.   Sandvika Camping

Sandvika campground provides a family-friendly campsite not far from Kabelvåg. The campground is open year and also contains cottages, flats, panoramic suites, and camping sites. Their showers and restrooms have been recently updated also.

Address: Ørsvågveien 45, 8310 Kabelvåg, Norway

14.   Hov Lofoten Camping

Hov Gård is a horseriding recreational complex with a nice restaurant and café that also provides camping.

The campground is close beside a nice sandy beach and you get excellent midnight sun here.

There are tent and campervan spots both with and without power. There are also showers and toilets.

You're incredibly near to Lofoten Links if you're in Lofoten for golfing. You may also hire the onsite sauna which is a terrific way to add a touch of relaxation to your stay.

Address: 8314 Gimsøysand, Norway

15.   Sandsletta Camping

Sandsletta was Lofoten's first campground and they give plenty of room for campers, campervans, and tents.

Coming close to its 60th anniversary, Sandsletta has a long history of offering services and meals. You may also organize trips and activities with Sandsletta.

The campsite's on-site restaurant serves coffee, lunches, cake, and supper so you do not need to cook under your tent or in your mobile home every night.

Address: Midnattsolveien 993, 8315 Laukvik, Norway

16.   Ramberg Camping Lofoten

Ramberg is a wonderful beach in Lofoten and you may camp in Ramberg Gjestegard where the sites are large.

There are showers, washrooms, and a kitchen as well as a restaurant on-site and a small store not too far away.

Camping in Ramberg begins at a nightly rate of 300 NOK at Sjøstrand Rorbuer & Fisk v/ Børge Iversen AS.

This moderately sized camping location near the harbor in Sjøstrand is excellently positioned for trekking. It's best for folks sleeping in a car rather than a tent considering its position.

The amenities are a little older than some of the other campgrounds on our list, but typically extremely well-maintained. Prices start at 150 NOK per night.

Address: 8380 Ramberg, Norway

Norway's Right to Roam - Dos and Don'ts

Norwegians enjoy the 'right to wander' which implies that people have the freedom to travel and camp on most territory in Norway.

However, this does not imply you have the right to camp exactly wherever you want or wander exactly anywhere you desire.

The freedom to wander works because Norwegians embrace the duties that are implicit in this act.

DO: Camp 150 meters away from the nearest inhabited home or cabin

DON'T: Don't Remain for more than 2 consecutive days.

DO: Comply with camping regulations and signposts

DON'T travel across land in quest of a wild camping spot DO follow Leave No Trace ethics

DO observe the Lofoten Code of Conduct

In 2021, Lofoten prohibited the ability to wander. Certain localities have rules in place that safeguard the land, animals, and lives of local citizens.

These include tent prohibitions at Reinebringen near Hamnøy Lofoten and portions of Haukland beach.

Top Tips for Camping in Lofoten, Norway

Before going camping in Lofoten there are several things you should keep in mind regarding Lofoten's weather and camping amenities to make sure you have a great experience.

Wind in Lofoten

Lofoten is renowned for being a windy location with variable weather. A mountain storm may come out of nowhere, particularly on the western shore which is open to the sea.

Bring a tent you've used previously in tough circumstances, not one you got for £10. You want to believe your tent is going to remain straight overnight and not try to fly off with you in it. When putting your tent up, make sure you've staked it out nicely so that it's nice and solid.

Check the ground carefully before setting up a tent

A lot of the ground in Lofoten is rather marshy. That's one of the reasons you'll find so many boardwalks on the treks out here.

If rain is anticipated, don't put your tent near the bottom of a hill, you'll probably wake up feeling a little moist.

Availability of water does mean it's frequently relatively simple to find water for drinking and cooking. There are several streams and lakes with pure drinking water all across Lofoten.

However, I would suggest filtering any water you save in this method through something like a Sawyer squeeze just in case.

Buying camping goods in Lofoten

Svolvaer and Leknes are the two main towns in Lofoten and offer lots of outdoor businesses where you can purchase camping equipment..

This includes propane for your camping stove because you can't fly with it if you fly to Lofoten, as well as anything you may have forgotten to take.

There are also numerous supermarkets throughout Lofoten where you may acquire food. Food in shops normally isn't too costly (a 5-pack of noodles is £1-2 and you can purchase bread for 70p)

Find your campground in Lofoten early

Lofoten is a bustling destination in the summer months and camping in Lofoten becomes crowded early in the day.

Try to select your campsite earlier in the day and then leave your tent or car/campervan if you don't need it there for the remainder of the day while you go exploring. That way you don't have to spend the whole evening seeking a free place.

I'd suggest you have a camping place secured by 5 pm at the latest in July/August.

Generally, you can't reserve a campground in Lofoten

While there may be occasional exceptions., most of the camping in Lofoten operates on a first-come, first-served basis.

That's why it's crucial to be there early in the day so you're not stuck driving about trying to locate someplace to sleep that night.

Lofoten campervan services and dump stations

Hopefully, this one is a no-brainer but make sure you utilize public garbage disposal if you're heading to Lofoten by campervan.

You should not and cannot dispose of your gray water on fields and roadways.

You may locate sani-dump stations, dispose of your garbage, use restrooms, and replenish water at the following sites.

Chapter 3

Local Cuisine in Lofoten Islands

Lofoten's rich heritage and history embrace more than simply fishing and gorgeous natural settings. Food and drink have long played an essential part in establishing Lofoten's identity. There is a varied selection of outstanding cuisine experiences to be found in Lofoten. You may be lured by a guided trip investigating the world of stockfish on the outlying islands of Røst. Or maybe you're interested in producing and enjoying your handmade cheese at Lofoten Gårdsysteri, a farm-based cheese factory.

The native gastronomy in Lofoten is inspired by the region's fishing background and the variety of seafood accessible in the surrounding seas. Some of the most popular local foods include Stockfish: Dried and salted cod has been a staple diet in Lofoten for ages.

- **Bacalao**: A classic Portuguese meal prepared with stockfish that has been modified to local preferences in Lofoten.

- **Fish soup:** A substantial soup cooked with a mix of fish and vegetables.

- **Reindeer meat:** A popular meat in the area, commonly eaten as a stew or in a traditional dish called "finnbiff".

- **Arctic char:** A species of freshwater fish found in the lakes and rivers of Lofoten, frequently eaten grilled or smoked.

- **Seafood platters:** A popular method to taste a range of local seafood, including shrimp, crab, scallops, and several species of fish.

In addition to these traditional foods, there are also numerous contemporary restaurants and cafés in Lofoten that offer a variety of world cuisine and fusion dishes, frequently employing local products.

Overall, the native cuisine in Lofoten is fresh, savory, and inspired by the region's natural resources and cultural past, giving it a unique and wonderful experience for tourists.

Top Restaurants and Cafes

Lofoten food studio

Lofoten Food Studio – a luxurious restaurant with stunning decorations in the Lofoten Islands, it is one of the restaurants in which the chef and his assistants prepare dishes in an open kitchen in front of visitors, to see their dishes during their preparation and smell the delicious aromas and mixing of ingredients in the restaurant yards. The restaurant provides a seasonal menu that varies with the seasons since the restaurant utilizes only fresh ingredients to produce the meals. Among the meals it provides there are pork with quail eggs, exquisite white asparagus, excellent crab, and many more.

Place address: Jacob Jentofts View 29, 8373 Ballstad, Norway

Gamle Skola Loknes

This café is a place for individuals searching for tasty cuisine at low prices. This café does not serve any regular foods, but rather a range of dishes, including vegetarian dishes, healthy dishes, and gluten-free dishes for those who desire. Among the foods he provides there is a superb cod fish sandwich, a grilled veggie sandwich, and a salami sandwich. The café also provides wonderful European pastries.

Place address: Grundstadveien 454, 8370 Leknes, Norway

Bringen Bringen

If you are a lover of European meals and you want to have a dinner that contains dishes from many European cuisines at the same time, this lovely restaurant offers you the most exquisite European dishes. Among the items it serves on the menu are steak on the French method, shrimp dish with tomato sauce on the Italian way, superb schnitzel on the German way, sausage on the Norwegian and German ways, and many more.

Place address: Reineveien 109, 8390 Reine, Norway

Restaurant Kjokkenet

This restaurant is situated in an area surrounded by ocean waves from all sides, and this spot creates a romantic ambiance suited for gatherings with loved ones. It is also a perfect restaurant for business meetings and big groups of people since it is quite spacious and has many huge tables. The restaurant provides typical Norwegian meals, which tourists will discover include pork stew, fried cinnamon sticks, grilled chicken, and many more.

Place address: Lamholmen, 8300 Svolvaer, Norway

Maren Anna

Maren Anna – This gorgeous café is one of the local favorites in Lofoten since it provides wonderful snacks and various fresh sandwiches, as well as pastries and baked goods that are cooked in the oven every morning. Among the meals he provides there are excellent potato stews served with mashed potatoes, avocado salad, smoked salmon salad, smoothies of various types, fudge cake, cheesecake, and many more.

Place address: Kaia, 8392 Sørvågen, Norway

8373 Cafe Ballstad *off route*

8373 Cafe Ballstad – This café is situated in a building that used to be a house, so guests will feel warm as soon as they approach the place since the people in charge of the café did not make any big alterations and retained the home environment within the place. It is a fairly big café that stretches across indoor and outdoor patios. The venue serves wonderful European foods that have been carefully picked to guarantee that all visitors' preferences are pleased. Among the foods presented are steak, lobster soup, burgers, waffles, and many more.

Place address: Øyaveien 99, 8373 Ballstad, Norway

Paleo Arctic

The culinary practices of Paleo Arctic on Lofoten Island, once essential for survival, are now preserved through generations, utilizing sea resources and mountain pastures. While no longer crucial for survival, these methods continue to uphold ancient culinary traditions. This restaurant exploits these approaches to the maximum to make excellent and delectable food for guests to the location. Although he makes food in traditional methods, he does not exhibit them in a very stunning contemporary style. Do not miss the chance to visit him!

The Address: Thon Hotel Lofoten Torget, 8300 Svolvær, Norway

Huset Kafe ~~Leknes~~

Huset Kafe – This cafe is one of the best cafes in the city for many reasons, the first of which is that it offers dishes that will suit all tastes of visitors, there are delicious oriental dishes such as hummus, vegetarian dishes such as Caesar salad and nachos, and French dishes such as smoked salmon sliders, and delicious desserts of all kinds. The second element that makes the café exceptional is its swift service and gorgeous furnishings that make the location appropriate for gatherings of friends and family.

The Address: Idrettsgata 1, 8370 Leknes, Norway

DIGG Restaurant

DIGG Restaurant – This restaurant provides numerous European grill delicacies on the menu and allows its clients the option to pick the additives and sauces they want for each dish, They offer a variety of dishes, including grilled beef ribs, tilapia, burgers, and more.The restaurant also gives its clients several vegetarian alternatives on the menu, as well as some halal options for its Muslim clientele.

Place address: Storgata 59, 8370 Leknes, Norway

Havet Restaurant

Havet Restaurant provides unique, internationally-inspired dishes by transforming ordinary ingredients into luxurious ones. Customers can enjoy possibly the best pizza or burger of their lives.And it is not limited to the components, as it also modifies the style of presentation to become more attractive and contemporary. Do not miss the chance to visit it since it is a restaurant that is well worth a visit!

Place address: Besselvågveien 8, 8392 Sørvågen, Norway

Borsen Spiseri

Borsen Spiseri – This restaurant is directed by a loving couple who wanted to introduce world-class cuisine to the city, and the meals in the restaurant are produced by a professional chef with decades of expertise in the area of cooking at the most recognized local restaurants. This restaurant boasts lovely outside terraces facing the ocean. The restaurant provides exquisite Norwegian cuisine, including grilled fish and steak, and the most renowned dish offered by the restaurant is the amazing grilled meat dish, which is produced from the finest varieties of fresh European meat.

Place address: Gunnar Bergs vei 2, 8300 Svolvær, Norway

Klatrekaféen

Klatrekaféen, a seaside cabin, features a delightful ambiance with diverse decorations and contrasting colors. Its large windows provide a direct view of the ocean, making it an ideal spot for a romantic dinner with the exceptional backdrop of waves hitting the exterior walls.On the menu, the business provides a fantastic shrimp sandwich accompanied by boiled eggs and lettuce, a beef dish served with mashed potatoes, burgers, and many more.

Place address: Misværveien 10, 8312 Henningsvær, Norway

Trygdekassen Galleri Og Kafe

Trygdekassen Gallery and Cafe serve delectable light dishes and hearty breakfasts, featuring items like waffles, pancakes, fudge desserts, and a variety of satisfying sandwiches, including omelet, salami, and smoked cheese. The restaurant offers its clients stunning outside terraces overlooking the Norwegian plains and the ocean, where tourists may enjoy the outdoors while enjoying their food.

Place address: E10 1270, 8392 Sørvågen, Norway

Krambua Restaurant

Krambua Restaurant - This restaurant is set in one of the ancient fishing cottages along the shore in Lofoten, and the location has décor that matches the character of the outside of the building, as the ceiling is covered with fishing nets and the walls are numerous giant stuffed fish. It is a restaurant where folks congregate to spend quality time with their friends and family. Among the foods he provides on the menu are grilled lobster pot, steak, burgers, and many more.

Place address: E10 180, 8390 Reine, Norway

Chapter 4

17 Outdoor Activities for both Summer and Winter that will give you an Awesome Experience

Norway's Lofoten Islands truly come alive in the summer, with long, bright days and nights suitable for staying outdoors and enjoying gorgeous scenery. During these summer months (May-August), travelers from all over the globe come to Lofoten to view the fjords, walk the mountains under the midnight sun, discover the little fishing communities, and experience the island's distinctive coastal culture and history.

In the winter, the northern lights flare across the sky, and the little red fishermen's cottages that cling to the snow-capped coastlines make for some wonderful picture motives. The brave travel out into the Lofoten wilderness for some spectacular skiing, snowboarding, or kayaking while the rest of us congregate in the modest coffee shops and galleries and wait for the northern lights.

Whether you're the adventurous kind seeking tough mountain treks or if your concept of adventure is more like browsing cozy shops, cafés, museums, and galleries, you'll find no lack of things to do in Lofoten. Lofoten has it all!

Lofoten's Spectacular Nature - The Fjords, Mountains & Beaches

There is no disputing that nature, seascape, beaches, fjords, and the magnificent light bring travelers to Lofoten from every part of the globe.

1. Take A Trollfjord Cruise

Taking a ship out to Trollfjord is Lofoten's most popular day excursion. A fjord tour is a fantastic opportunity to view the Lofoten Islands, water, and shoreline that encourages people to dwell along this coast.

All the Trollfjord cruises start at Svolvaer port and will take you to view the legendary Trollfjord, Lofoten's most stunning fjord. The fjord is noted for its steep and narrow entry (approximately 100 meters wide), flanked by lofty mountains. Trollfjord can only be accessed by boat.

Several sorts of Trollfjord cruises are offered, from entertaining high-speed rib trips (2 hours) to slower-paced tours that take a bit longer but give you more time to admire the views.

Silent Hybrid-Electric Ship Trollfjord Cruise (3.5 hours).
We had a Trollfjord trip aboard the new electric ship Brim Explorer and liked it! We believe it's the greatest way to visit Trollfjord. This route begins and concludes at Svolvær.
Season: mid-April – 8. October

Explore Trollfjord on a 2-hour RIB-Boat Sea Eagle Safari.
From Svolvær, you may also join a Sea Eagle Safari cruise to Trollfjord. The trips are via high-speed rib boat. While they also wind up at Trollfjord, they focus just as much on viewing the spectacular sea eagles.
Season: All year

1295 00 kroner

Luxury Sailing Yacht From Svolvaer To Trollfjord (5 hours)

See Trollfjord aboard the lovely sailing vessel S/Y Stella Oceana. This is a 100-foot (32-meter) antique boat, and the skipper is a former Norwegian Coast Guard Sea skipper so you will be in safe hands. The boat features two outdoor decks and one internal saloon where you will be given traditional reindeer soup with fresh bread, coffee, tea, hot chocolate, and cookies for lunch. The yacht also features an outdoor hot tub on deck, which you may use for an additional cost. What is more soothing than watching the Trollfjord and sea eagles from the hot tub?!

Season: May – 1. October

Embark on a 13-hour Lofoten day excursion with Hurtigruten, including a visit to Trollfjord, starting from Svolvær.

Hurtigruten is like an institution in Norway and has been sailing around the whole Norwegian coast from Bergen to Kirkenes since 1893. This excursion is a terrific opportunity to enjoy the Hurtigruten sail from Svolvaer to Stokmarknes, one of the most picturesque portions of the whole Hurtigruten journey. Along the route, you will cruise across Trollfjord. This day's journey begins and concludes at Svolvær. In Stokmarknes, you will have the opportunity to see the brand-new Hurtigruten Museum and explore Stokmarknes town.

Season: May – mid-August

2. Go Fjord Fishing

Another popular and great way to explore the seascape surrounding Lofoten is to embark on a fishing expedition in the fjords and Arctic Sea that surrounds Lofoten. Fishing is a huge part of Norwegian culture, and going fishing is a pleasant way to view the lovely Lofoten countryside.

Lofoten is one of the greatest locations to go fishing in Norway since it is famed for its fish, particularly cod. You are nearly always certain to obtain some fish in Lofoten, most likely cod, pollock, haddock, mackerel, and halibut.

From Svolvær: Traditional Fishing Trip (4 hours)

On this fishing excursion, you will get to go fishing aboard the classic and beautiful wooden Norwegian fishing boat MS Symra. The ship sails from Svolvaer port and returns around 4 hours later.

The crew will give you everything you need, including a fishing outfit, safety equipment like a thermal suit, and a floating vest. In addition, there is an English-speaking guide on board that will offer you pointers on how to fish.

Season: April – 1. November

Indulge in a 3-hour luxury fishing experience in the Lofoten Islands departing from Svolvær.

Join this fishing expedition for a delightful 3-hour fjord sail aboard the beautiful ship S/Y Stella Oceana. The boat features two outer decks and a big internal saloon. This is a small-group excursion with a limit of 12 individuals. A local, passionate, English-speaking (also speaks Japanese), and very skilled fishing guide will tell you all about how to catch some fish. All fishing equipment is supplied aboard. A vegetable soup with freshly baked bread, combined with coffee, tea, hot cocoa, water & cookies, will be provided abroad throughout the voyage. And if you catch a fish (which you most likely will…), it may be added to your soup, or you can take it with you back home.

Season: April – mid-September

Explore the Lofoten Islands with an 8-hour fishing and fjord cruise from Svolvær, including lunch.

The aforementioned fishing excursion aboard S/Y Stella Oceana may also be organized as a full-day tour (8 hours), where you get to embark on a longer fjord cruise in Lofoten while fishing along the way. On this tour, you get to enjoy the outdoor hot tub on the terrace and be served lunch (reindeer soup with root vegetables & freshly baked bread), snacks, coffee, tea, hot chocolate, and cookies. In the afternoon, you will be given supper, which is your self-caught fish.

Season: May – mid-August

3. Marvel At The Northern Lights

In recent years Lofoten has become increasingly renowned as a superb site for witnessing the northern lights.

The northern lights are visible in Lofoten in the winter months from September to April. Most visitors like to come in February & March when there is more sunshine and warmer temperatures, however, the evenings are still dark enough to watch the amazing lights flash across the sky.

While Tromso still draws more northern light seekers, there is something special about viewing the northern lights flashing over Lofoten's distinctive environment with its traditional towns and rorbuer/ fishermen's huts.

You may go to the northern lights chasing on your own or join a trip. The benefit of taking a trip is that the tour leaders are experts in interpreting the weather and the northern lights prediction and know the region. So you will normally have a higher chance of seeing the northern lights on a tour, particularly if you are short on time and just intend on spending a few days in Lofoten.

Embark on a 5-hour Northern Lights chase with a professional photographer, starting from Svolvaer.

This 5-hour northern lights trip is in a small group (max 8 persons), where your guide is a talented photographer. During this trip, you will not only witness the northern lights (if you are fortunate) but also learn how to snap beautiful shots of the dancing lights. You get to borrow a tripod (which is necessary for capturing those crisp northern lights photographs) and learn the settings on your camera. This trip begins at Svolvaer.

Season: 1. September – 1. April

Experience a 4-hour Northern Lights cruise from Svolvær paired with a local tasting menu.

Why not combine witnessing the Northern Lights with a fjord cruise while eating great local delicacies from Lofoten? Yep, on this trip, you get to do all three. This 4-hour fjord tour aboard the modern and pleasant electric ship Brim Explorer takes you from Svolvaer into the fjord Austnesfjorden, west via the settlement of Henningsvær, or south across the islands of Skrova and Lille Molla. Along the way, you will be given a superb tasting menu supper prepared of local delicacies from Lofoten in the pleasant and warm interior saloon with panoramic views. A passionate local English-speaking guide will share anecdotes along the trip about the sites you sail by and the meals you get served.

Season: 1. February – 1. April

4. Have A Scenic Picnic At Ramberg Beach

Ramberg Beach is Lofoten's longest beach and one of the most picturesque. It's an excellent area to stop for a breather on your drive through Lofoten as the major road runs next to it. You can't miss it.

We enjoyed a beautiful lunch on the Ramberg beach with freshly made bread from the local bakery in Svolvær and goat cheese from the local Lofoten Gårdsysteri and watched the kite surfers play on the lake.

If you feel like performing some water activities, Ramberg is where Kari Skibevåg, a former world champion Kite surfer from Norway, has founded her adventure firm. She currently takes guests out for scuba diving, kite surfing, and surfing.

Ramberg is also a popular area to camp as it contains one of the biggest campgrounds in Lofoten, a store, and a few charming cafés.

5. Enjoy The Midnight Sun

The period of the midnight sun in Lofoten spans from May 28 to July 14. July. These months the sun is up day and night; it never goes dark.

To view the midnight sun in Lofoten, take a night trek to the west coast, where the sun lingers over the North Sea but never drops below the horizon or behind the mountains. Some outstanding sites to watch the midnight sun in Lofoten include:

- Eggum
- Unstad
- Uttakleiv
- Gimsøy

If you don't have a vehicle, the easiest way to watch the midnight sun is to take a tour that includes hotel pick up and drop off, like these two:

From Svolvaer: Midnight Sun Photography Tour (4 hours)

This journey brings you to the greatest sites to observe the midnight sun in Lofoten, on the outer Atlantic coast. A professional photographer and tour leader will teach you how to shoot excellent midnight sunshots. If you don't have a camera, you may use your cell phone, and your guide will give you his images taken during the tour. The guide will take you up to your hotel in Svolvaer or Kabelvaag at 21:00/ 9 pm, and you will be back at your hotel by 01:00. You may pick this trip in English, Italian, and Spanish.

Season: 11. May – 1. August

Embark on a 3-hour sailing tour to witness the midnight sun in the Lofoten Islands, departing from Svolvær.

This 3-hour sailing excursion takes you on a midnight sun sailing voyage aboard a luxury sailing yacht. Enjoy the midnight sun and the sea wind on your hair from one of the two outside decks. Along the route, you will get breathtaking views of fjords, high mountains, and unspoiled beaches, all coated in the golden light of the Midnight Sun. Hopefully, you will also get to view some wildlife like eagles, puffins, dolphins, and whales. The Stella Oceana ship also includes an outdoor hot tub on deck if you want to warm up and thoroughly relax. You will be provided refreshments including coffee, tea, hot chocolate, water, and pastries. The yacht also includes a huge inside saloon. Your passionate local English-speaking guide will share anecdotes along the journey about the things and places you visit and also point out animals. The boat leaves at 17:30/ 5:30 pm, and you will be back in Svolvaer at 20:30/ 8:30 pm. You may pick this trip in English, Norwegian, and Japanese.

Season: mid-May – mid-August

Relax On Some Of Europe's Best Beaches

It may surprise you that Lofoten is famed for its stunning beaches, but it truly is.

6. **Haukland Beach**

Haukland has even been awarded the greatest beach in Europe. A popular and picturesque trek in Haukland is the 1,5 km long climb to the peak Mannen (400 m tall).

While the ocean temperature can never rival beaches in southern Europe or even south Norway, the beaches themselves are spectacular. Long golden sand beaches may make you entirely forget you are above the Arctic Circle on a bright day. Until you attempt to get in the water, that is.

Some of the most magnificent beaches in Lofoten, in addition to Haukland Beach, are Ramberg Beach, Unstad Beach, Uttakleiv Beach, Horseid Beach, Bunes Beach, Gimsøy Beach, Rørvika Beach, and Kvalvika Beach.

Explore Haukland Beach on a 7-hour summer photography tour in the Lofoten Islands.
This tour takes you on a day excursion to Lofoten's most renowned beach — Haukland Beach. You also get to visit other gorgeous sites like Eggum, Kabelvåg, Henningsvær, and Unstad Beach. This trip begins in the Svolvær/ Kabelvåg region.
Season: May – 1. October

Ready for some of Lofoten's most sought-after activities? Ready for a challenge?

Lofoten's stunning blend of rocky mountains and fjords means that it is a magnet for outdoor sports. People from all over the globe come here to climb and trek the mountains, surf the waves, golf, or explore the seascape.

7. Go Fjord Kayaking

Kayaking is a popular activity in Lofoten and a terrific opportunity to see the Lofoten coastline.

Some guesthouses and rorbuer offer kayaks accessible for visitors to use and organize trips, such as the magnificent Catogården in Reine.

You may join a kayaking guided trip from numerous areas in Lofoten, including Svolvær, Kabelvåg, and Eggum. Some of the most popular kayaking trips in Lofoten are:

Svolvær: Evening Kayaking Adventure (2 hours)
This Kayaking trip begins in Svolvær, and you'll paddle around the picturesque Svolvær coast for approximately 2

hours. The English-speaking guide will explain and relate anecdotes about the culture and history of the region. No prior kayaking experience is necessary. All equipment is provided.

Season: 1. June – mid-August

Embark on a kayaking adventure in Eggum ranging from 3 to 7 hours.

This kayaking excursion begins at Eggum in Lofoten, and you get to explore the Arctic Sea and the gorgeous coastline of Lofoten. The guide will give you everything you need to enjoy a pleasant and comfortable kayaking adventure, and no prior kayaking experience is essential. You may pick a half-day (3 hours) full-day kayaking excursion (7 hours) or a midnight sun tour in the evening (3 hours).

Season: 15. May – 1. November

8. Hike Lofoten's Spectacular Mountains

Top Hiking Trails in Lofoten Island

Lofoten is recognized as a hikers' paradise with steep, craggy mountains that rise majestically from narrow fjords, providing breathtaking vistas. No matter your expertise level, you may discover some wonderful walks here.

Here's where to discover the greatest hiking in Lofoten:

Håen Hike

- Distance: 3.2km (2 mi) one way
- Difficulty: easy
- Time: 1.5 hours to the summit
- Parking: Håen parking lot
- Trailhead: Håen parking lot
- Address: 8063 Værøy, Norway

Håen, also known as Håheia, is a picturesque high peak on the lonely island of Værøy. It boasts one of the most bizarre vistas in all of Lofoten and is a very moderate trek, at least by Norwegian standards.

To reach Værøy island, you may take the free ferry from Bodø or Moskenes. The starting point and parking lot for the Håen trek are located northwest of the hamlet of Sørland and designated as 'Håen Parkering' on Google Maps.

To get to the peak of Håen, you may either walk practically the whole way up on an old paved military road or take one of the paths on either side of the road. Once you're at the top, you'll have to go past a radar station to get to the overlook beyond it.

There you'll be rewarded with awe-inspiring views of the whole western peninsula of Værøy and its green mountains, neon blue ocean, and white sand beach. It's the type of spot that will make you feel like you've arrived at the end of the planet. This was probably one of the highlights of my Lofoten tour and one of my favorite perspectives in all of Lofoten.

Reinebringen Hike

- Distance: 1.4km (0.9 mi) one way
- Difficulty: medium
- Time: 1 hour to the summit
- Parking: Steffenakken parking lot or the outer port of Reine
- Trailhead: Southern end of Ramsvik Tunnel

- Address: Moskenesøya, Moskenes, Norway

The trek to the summit of Reinebringen is frequently regarded as one of the greatest hikes in Lofoten - and justifiably so! Located near the hamlet of Reine, this 448m (1470 ft) tall mountain is reasonably simple to ascend and has a fantastic perspective of the gorgeous Reinefjord and the spectacular peaks surrounding it.

Although the route leading to the peak of Reinebringen is short, it is rather steep and involves ascending 1978 stone steps. These stairs were erected by Nepalese Sherpas during the years 2016-2021 to make it safer for visitors to perform this renowned Lofoten climb and to safeguard the earth from erosion.

It is only suggested to trek Reinebringen from May to September. As it's a hugely popular trek, you can expect to see many people on the route in the summer months. But if you undertake the climb later in the evening – which is a terrific idea during the Midnight Sun time – you could have the spot to yourself as we did.

Festvågtind Hike

- Distance: 1.9km (1.2 mi) one way
- Difficulty: medium

- Time: 1-1.5 hours to the summit
- Parking: Festvågtind parking lot
- Trailhead: 300m (0.2 km) east of Festvågtind parking
- Address: Henningsværveien 51, 8312 Henningsvær, Norway

Rising 541m (1775 ft) above the sea, Festvågtind is yet another popular summit walk on the Lofoten Islands. The mountain stands on the island of Austvågøya, directly adjacent to the fishing community of Henningsvær, which is a major tourist attraction in Lofoten.

The route up to the summit is rocky and pretty steep and may become a little muddy if it's been raining. At the peak, however, your efforts will be rewarded with a stunning 360-degree panorama of the surrounding environment and the settlement of Henningsvær spread out on little islands.

On a day with excellent sights, you can even see mainland Norway from here. This top is also a fantastic site for seeing the Midnight Sun.

On your way back down, I suggest making a stop at the Heiavatnet Lake, which is around halfway down the route. In the summer, you may go for an invigorating plunge in the lake's icy waters. It's the ideal way to chill off after this tough journey.

Torsketunga Hike (Presten)

- Distance: 2.6km (1.6 mi) one way
- Difficulty: medium/hard
- Time: 1.5-2 hours to the summit
- Parking: Festvågtind parking lot
- Trailhead: 300m (0.2 km) east of Festvågtind parking
- Address: Henningsværveien 51, 8312 Henningsvær, Norway

Torsketunga, commonly known as Preston, is one of the top treks in Lofoten for people searching for an adrenaline rush. It has a spectacular outlook and is one of the greatest picture sites in Lofoten — a slab of granite that juts out of the slope and has a precipitous drop below it. From here, you may enjoy beautiful views of fjords, mountains, and the blue water. Although the climb to Torsketunga is practically simply an extension of the famed Festvågtind hike, it nonetheless remains a hidden treasure and hardly attracts any hikers. This is most likely owing to the fairly difficult access to the perspective.

The path includes several exposed spots with practically vertical drops adjacent to it and a few areas that require a little rock climbing. Because of this, I only advocate undertaking the Torsketunga trek if you're not terrified of heights and are secure in your ability to climb a few meters.

I'm going to be honest — there were a few times towards the conclusion of my trip when I was a little apprehensive to continue and was questioning if it was truly safe. I'd 100% do it again however since it was worth all the work! You simply have to be extra attentive.

Ryten & Kvalvika Beach Hike

- Distance: 7km (4.3 mi) (to the peak and the beach)
- Difficulty: medium
- Time: 3-3.5 hours (to the mountain and the beach)
- Parking: Innersand Parking
- Trailhead: Innersand Parking
- Address: Fv806 7, 8387 Fredvang, Norway

The path to the peak of Ryten and Kvalvika Beach is another one of the greatest Lofoten hiking trails, drawing hundreds of hikers and outdoor lovers throughout the summer. Rising to a height of 543m (1782 ft), the top of Ryten affords a beautiful view of Kvalvika Beach below.

The remote Kvalvika Beach is regarded as one of the most beautiful beaches in Lofoten and is a favorite site for wild camping. Nestled between steep mountains that rise directly from the water, this exotic beach is only accessible by foot.

There are a variety of different pathways you may follow to get to Kvalvika and Ryten. We selected the one beginning from Innersand since it has the biggest parking lot but you may also start from the Torsfjorden side. Unfortunately, we didn't witness the famed bird's-eye-view of the coastline from Ryten since the mountain was enveloped in heavy clouds while we were there.

Although this trip is by far the longest hike on our list, it's not particularly demanding or steep and can be done by anybody with a respectable fitness level. Kvalvika Beach and Ryten are accessible even during the winter although you may require hiking crampons or snowshoes.

Mannen Hike

- Distance: 2km (1.2 mi) one way
- Difficulty: easy
- Time: <1 hour to the summit
- Parking: Haukland Beach parking lot
- Trailhead: Across the road from the parking lot
- Address: Uttakleivveien 200, 8370 Leknes, Norway

Mannen is a tiny mountain top overlooking the postcard-perfect Haukland Beach, one of the nicest beaches in

Lofoten. The trek to its peak is brief but quite rewarding and gives a great perspective of the surrounding region. You'll probably also encounter some adorable lambs along the road.

With the grassy meadows, chalk-white beaches, blue ocean, and mountains in the backdrop, the view from the summit of Mannen truly shows off the spectacular natural beauty of Lofoten.

Although Mannen is regarded as one of the simplest walks in Lofoten, I wouldn't say it's exactly a stroll in the park. The path is constantly uphill and might be muddy after rain. As you approach closer to the peak, the route meanders around the crest of the mountain and has some exposed places where you have to be cautious.

During our trek, it was incredibly windy at the summit of Mannen. Bring a windbreaker!

Offersøykammen Hike

- Distance: 1.3km (0.8 mi)
- Difficulty: easy/medium
- Time: <1 hour to the summit
- Parking: 'Skreda – Nasjonale Turistveger' rest stop
- Trailhead: Across the road from Lofothytter
- Address: 8370 Leknes, Norway

This is a simple climb by Lofoten standards but for the ordinary person, the more realistic assessment would probably be medium hard. Although the trip is brief, it's a hard and steady ascent straight up the slope with an elevation gain of 436m (1430 feet).

Once you've made your way to the summit, you may enjoy unrestricted 360-degree views of the distinctive beauty of the Lofoten Islands. On one side, you'll witness enormous swampy lowlands covered with ponds, and on the other, mountains and bays with green water.

It's ideal to undertake the Offersøykammen climb on a clear bright day since the vistas will be a lot more amazing and the scenery will seem more vibrant.

We conducted the trek via the short and steep path. However, there's also the option of following a longer and flatter trekking path, which begins immediately before the Nappstraum tunnel. From there, the trek to the peak takes around 2 hours.

9. See The Lofoten Islands From A Bicycle

Lofoten is a great region to explore with a bicycle. The next town or guesthouse is seldom too far away, and although it is rather mountainous in spots, the gorgeous countryside makes up for the hard effort.

If you wish to explore Lofoten by bike, plan wisely and be ready for unexpected poor weather.

10.   Go Horseback Riding

At Hov Farm in Gimsøy, you may enjoy horseback riding. Their most popular tour is a short journey that is also suited for individuals with no equestrian riding expertise. But they may also offer lengthier multi-day tours for more experienced individuals.

11.Stay In A Traditional Rorbu/ Fisherman's Cabin

The unique little red wooden houses that adorn the Lofoten shoreline have become world-famous. I would argue that you have not truly visited Lofoten if you have not slept at least one night in a fisherman's cottage.

When Lofoten's fishing business was at its pinnacle, tens of thousands of fishermen would flock to Lofoten to engage in the winter cod fishery. To keep near to the water and the boats, small shelters were erected where the crew could eat and sleep. In Norwegian, we call such a cabin a "rorbu".

Today, the fishing boats have space for the fishermen to sleep aboard the boat, and many of the huts have been converted into leisure cottages and are available for rent. Staying in a rorbu for a night or longer is something you should do while visiting Lofoten.

From the exterior, they all appear more or less the same with their unique red and white coloring, but on the inside, they may vary substantially. Some are fairly rudimentary, but others, like the one below at Nusfjord Arctic Resort, have been wonderfully renovated into luxurious accommodations with every convenience.

Our favorite rorbuer/ fisherman's cottages in Lofoten are:

- Nusfjord Arctic Resort – The cutest Hattvika Lodge in Ballstad – The most elegant
- Eliassen Rorbuer in Reine – The most gorgeous and Instagram-famous
- The yellow cabins at Sakrisøy Rorbuer in Reine.
- Svinøya Rorbuer in Svolvaer - The most lovely
- Nyvågar Robuhotell in Kabelvåg - Great location

12. Mountain Skiing & Snowshoeing

In the winter (from February to April) and when the weather conditions are appropriate, Lofoten becomes a mountain skiing, snowboarding, and snowshoeing hotspot.

Some of the greatest mountains for skiing include Geitgalljene (demanding, for experienced skiers), Torskmannen (medium), Blåtinden (medium), and Småtindan (easy, for all abilities).

The Lofoten mountains may be perilous, and the weather can change in an instant, so I'd suggest traveling with a local guide from, for instance, North Norwegian Climbing School in Henningsvær or Lofoten Ski Lodge.

From Svolvær: Snowshoe Nature Explorer (3 hours)

On this 3-hour excursion, an enthusiastic local English-speaking mountain guide takes you snowshoe trekking in the highlands near Svolvaer. You will trek through some of the most gorgeous mountain locations with breathtaking vistas. Snowshoes and poles are supplied, but you must wear warm winter gear. You will be provided something warm to drink along the journey.

Season: November – mid-April

14. Snowshoe hiking trip

Private Snowshoeing Excursion in Lofoten (3 hours)

If you are a group or family of at least four individuals, this is a wonderful chance to go snowshoeing with a private guide. The guide will pick you up at your accommodation in Lofoten (where it is) and will transport you to the hiking location. The snowshoeing trip will take you through the picturesque Lofoten landscape, through the forests, fjords, and frozen lakes. The excursion includes transport from and back to your accommodation, expert mountain guides, refreshments, and hot beverages. The degree of the exercise as well as the time is adapted to your fitness level and desires.

15. Surf At Unstad Beach

Lofoten is highly recognized for its outstanding surfing conditions. The conditions are ideal throughout the autumn and winter, but if you are a novice, the smaller waves during the summer can be excellent for you.

Most of the surfing activity takes place at Unstad Beach on the west coast, where a committed group of surfers rides the waves pouring in from the endless North Sea.

You may hire a board here and have a try, or stay at Unstad Surf Camp for a few days, take a surf lesson, and learn from the masters.

By the way, if you're traveling to look at the surf, stop at Unstad Surf Camp and taste their famous cinnamon pastries! They are incredibly excellent.

16. Learn To Mountain Climb

The tiny fishing town Henningsvær is regarded as Lofoten's hub of mountain climbing and bouldering.

Nord Norsk Klatreskole is the major center for climbing in Lofoten and is an excellent location to start if you are interested in mountain climbing and bouldering in Lofoten. They organize climbing classes and also hire out climbing gear.

Oh, and by the way, don't miss the nice café next door, Henningsvær's renowned Klatrekafeen

17. Trekking and Rappel Excursion in Eggum

This is a wonderful trekking/rappel excursion to Eggum, on the north shore of Lofoten. You may select a half-day or a full-day adventure. You either kayak or trek (depending on the weather and your interests) to the Rock Wall, where you will rappel a 20 m path. The guides are skilled and trained mountain climbers and hikers and will give you a comprehensive safety briefing and offer you all the essential equipment. No requirement for prior rappelling/kayaking/trekking experience; this is for novices also.

Season: 1. May – 1. October

Top Tourist Attractions in Lofoten Island that you wouldn't want to miss for anything in the World

Svolvaer

Lofoten's biggest town, Svolvaer has a population of 4,720 and is situated on the south coast of Austvågøy. Well connected by ferries and cruise ships from the mainland and internationally, this town is a key fishing harbor and is where most travelers begin their Lofoten trip.

Svolvaer is a bustling destination to explore, particularly around the port area with its many good cafés, pubs, and restaurants. In addition to its stores and galleries, there are a lot of wonderful cultural institutions worth seeing, too.

Topping the list are the Lofoten War Memorial Museum with its exhibitions linked to the wartime occupation and Magic

Ice. The latter is a unique environment where Lofoten's life is represented in ice sculptures. You'll also want to visit the North Norwegian Artist's Centre, which offers a continually changing selection of artwork in diverse mediums.

The Svolvær Goat Trail

If you're a hiker or a mountain climber (or probably a little of both), check out the famed Svolvær Goat (Svolværgeita).

This remarkable twin-peaked granite outcrop is visible from downtown Svolvaer and provides amazing views for anyone daring enough to make the renowned "Svolvær Goat Leap." This dangerous 1.5-meter jump surely isn't for the faint of heart, but it's not rare if you do reach the summit, to witness the odd skilled climber accomplish it.

Although the difficult climb to the foot of the mountain takes less than an hour, the services of a professional guide are highly suggested for anyone hoping to make their way to the summit. If it's on your bucket list, prepare to spend roughly four hours all told, including the walk, the climb, and rappelling back down this spectacular rock structure.

Lofotr Viking Museum

The Lofotr Viking Museum (Lofotr Vikingmuseum) in Bøstad on the island of Vestvågøy is a must-visit while in the Lofotens. The centerpiece is a replica of the 272-foot-long chieftain's residence, the longest Viking-era edifice on record, that formerly stood on the site about 500 CE.

This wonderful Viking experience includes a superb short video about the lives of the chieftain and his family, as well as explanatory tours of the home and the various items uncovered on the site during archeological investigations.
Afterward, stroll down to the nearby lake to admire the replica Viking warships, including an outstanding longship. If coming

in August, make sure to catch the Lofotr Viking Festival, which features re-enactments and the opportunity to witness magnificent Viking warships at sea. A café and museum store are available on-site.

Address: Vikingveien 539, 8360 Bøstad

Trollfjord

From the straits of Raftsund, a tiny, rocky passage allows access to the Trollfjord, one of Lofoten's most popular tour boat trips. Towering above the fjord are the snowcapped Higravtinder (1,191 meters) and the craggy Trolltinder (1,045 meters) mountains, both standing high above the Trollfjord.

This beautiful 3.2-kilometer-long alpine lake is normally frozen over.

Another popular day excursion is via bus from Svolvőr to Stokmarknes and returning by the express boat, which cruises along the Trollfjord. Only 800 meters at its broadest, it is quite the sight to witness cruise ships squeeze through the small gap during the summer months.

Kabelvåg

Kabelvåg, a little fishing community on Austvågøy, is a fantastic site to learn more about the significance of fishing in Lofoten. Start with the Lofoten Museum (Lofotmuseet) with its exhibitions of life in the 1800s, including the history of fishing on the islands, a collection of Nordland-type boats, and authentic fishermen's homes.

The Lofoten Aquarium (Lofotakvariet) is well worth a visit. This popular site allows learning more about the area's marine biodiversity, including fish and sea creatures from Lofoten. Finally, make sure to go visit Vågan Church, the biggest wooden church north of Trondheim.

Aquarium Address: Storvåganveien 28, 8310 Kabelvåg

Røst Island

Accessible only by boat, the spectacular Røst Island (Røstlandet), situated approximately 99 kilometers off the mainland, is home to a vast colony of seabirds, including over three million puffins. Thanks to its seclusion, the island's steep crags, called Vedøy, Storfjell, Stavøy, and Nykan, are suitable habitats for numerous uncommon species, such as the larger and lesser storm petrels and fulmars.

All in all, a fourth of Norway's seabird population resides on the island, a statistic that makes the voyage by boat from Røstland all the more worthwhile. As a consequence of this richness of species, most of the island has been declared a conservation reserve.

While there, make sure to also see the Skomvaer Lighthouse (Skomvær fyr). Built in 1887, it's regarded to be the Lofoten's most isolated Atlantic outpost.

Å

You might say all roads lead to Å, Lofoten's most westerly point. In addition to its beautiful vistas, this settlement on the island of Moskenesøy is home to the Norwegian Fishing Settlement Museum (Norsk Fiskeværsmuseum).

Exhibits include a functioning forge and stone oven bakery, the typical residence of a fisherman, and traditional boats, as well as a gift store with locally created items, like cod liver oil produced directly at the museum.

Afterward, visit the Lofoten Stockfish Museum (Lofoten Tørrfiskmuseum) devoted to Lofoten's most renowned, thousand-year-old export. Made from the copious cod that spawn in Lofoten's shallow seas, stockfish is omnipresent on the islands, allowed to cure throughout the colder months on many drying racks, and forms the foundation for many of Lofoten's superb fish dishes.

Address: Å vegen 5, 8392 Sørvågen

Reine

Often recognized as the most beautiful hamlet in Norway, Reine, which translates as "Queen," is a charming fishing settlement situated on Moskenesøy. This prominent tourist site has long been a favorite haunt of artists and climbers because of its breathtaking fjord and mountain vistas.

The high elevation above the settlement affords great views of the Moskenesstrømmen, a maelstrom described by Jules Verne and Edgar Allan Poe and regarded as one of the strongest such whirlpools in the world. For a close-up view of the maelstrom, join one of the numerous exhilarating boat tours through Moskenstraumen.

Address: Reine, Moskenesøy

Rorbuer: Fishing Huts

For a memorable experience, treat yourself to a stay in one of Lofoten's distinctive red fishing huts. Perched high above the tidal waves in various fishing settlements surrounding Lofoten, several of these "rorbuer" (or "sjøhus") have been turned into hotels and are suitable for use as a base to explore the region.

Originally erected to offer modest overnight shelter for fishermen, many of these wharf houses, generally two or three stories high, are now available for rent. Accommodations vary from basic, which includes a few bunks and a stove, to elegant fully catered suites.

Glasshytta: The Glassblower at Vikten Leknes

Northern Norway's first glassblower, artist Åsvar Tangrand, started to make blown glass artwork and products after being inspired by the magnificent surrounding terrain of Vikten. Tangrand's work immediately became renowned across Norway for the methods he devised and his distinctive sign "Lofotruna."

The studio, entitled Glasshytta, is a fascinating complex of linked buildings that are worth seeing even if you're not in the market for glassware. The studio is also home to a pottery

116

workshop, as well as a pleasant coffee shop, and tourists may explore the grounds.

Address: Gnr 34 Bnr 22, 8382 Napp

Lofoten War Memorial Museum

The Lofoten War Memorial Museum (Lofoten Krigsminnemuseum) is highly worth seeing for military fans and history lovers alike. This intriguing museum displays a substantial collection of WWII-era uniforms and memorabilia relating to the WWII period and the Nazi occupation of the islands.

In addition to exhibits showing the role of the Norwegian resistance, it also contains exhibitions about the life of regular residents under the German occupation.

Address: Fiskergata 3, 8300 Svolvær, Norway

Chapter 5

Cultural Experiences- Festivals and events

Lofoten Islands hold several festivals and events throughout the year, promoting the region's culture, music, and outdoor sports. Here are some prominent ones:

- **Lofoten International Chamber Music Festival:** - Celebrating classical music, this festival brings together international and local performers, giving performances in unusual places around the islands.

- **Lofoten Food Festival (Matfestivalen):-** Showcasing local cuisine and culinary traditions, this festival draws food aficionados with tastings, seminars, and activities showcasing regional delicacies.

- **Lofoten International Art event (LIAF):-** This contemporary art event shows installations, performances, and exhibitions at different venues, contributing to Lofoten's developing cultural environment.

- **Lofoten Foreign Film Festival (LIFF):** - Film aficionados come to enjoy a broad variety of foreign and local films, typically exhibited in unorthodox venues.

- **Fishing contests:-** Given Lofoten's fishing background, different fishing contests take place, drawing competitors and spectators alike.

- **Midnight Sun Marathon:** - Held in Svolvær, this marathon makes use of the midnight sun, delivering a unique running experience throughout the summer months.

- **Lofoten Viking Festival:** - Embrace Viking history and culture via reenactments, seminars, and demonstrations, providing an insight into Lofoten's historical origins.

- **Lofoten Worldwide Literature Festival:-** Literature aficionados meet to celebrate Nordic and worldwide literature via readings, talks, and book releases.

It's important to verify the festival dates and program information closer to your trip dates, since they may alter from year to year. Attending these events may offer a rich cultural layer to your Lofoten vacation.

.

Chapter 6

Shopping on Lofoten Island

Lofoten Gaver og Brukskunst (Gifts and Applied Art):-

Location: Storgata 38, 8370 Leknes, Norway

Details: This business in Svolvær provides a range of local arts and crafts, including textiles, pottery, and jewelry.

Fiskekrogen:

Location: Dreyers gate 29, 8312 Henningsvær, Norway

Details: A store in Svolvær recognized for its variety of high-quality apparel, accessories, and gifts inspired by the sea and fishing tradition.

Galleri Lofoten:

Location: Misværveien 18, 8312 Henningsvær, Norway

Details: An art gallery in Henningsvær where you may acquire paintings, sculptures, and other artworks made by local and worldwide artists.

Lofoten Wool (Lofoten Ull):

Location: Various stores over Lofoten, notably Svolvær and Henningsvær.

Details: Offers locally created wool items such as sweaters, blankets, and accessories.

Fiskarjentas Hus (Fisherman's Daughter):

Location: Henningsvær

Details: This store in Henningsvær provides a mix of local and Scandinavian design items, apparel, and accessories.

Lofoten Glass AS:

Location: Steinveien 15, 8310 Kabelvåg, Norway

Details: A glassblowing workshop in Vikten where you may acquire unique glass art manufactured on-site.

Svolvær Market Square:

Location: Torget 18-22, 8300 Svolvær, Norway

Details: Check around the market area for kiosks offering local vegetables, crafts, and souvenirs, particularly during events and festivals.

Lofoten Handicraft (Lofoten Husflid)

Location: Flakstadveien 489, 8380 Ramberg, Norway

Details: A store providing traditional Norwegian goods, including handcrafted textiles, woodwork, and jewelry.

Remember that the availability of items may vary, and it's always a good idea to visit local markets and smaller stores for hidden treasures and true Lofoten experiences.

Nightlife in Lofoten Island

While Lofoten Islands may not have a booming nightlife scene like bigger towns, there are a few particular pubs and bars where you may have a drink and a relaxing environment. Keep in mind that the options may fluctuate.

Bacalao Bar

Location: Torget 23, 8300 Svolvær, Norway

Details:Bacalao Bar is another choice in Svolvær, noted for its dynamic atmosphere and a selection of cocktails. It's a nice location to relax in the evening.

Remember that the nightlife in the Lofoten Islands tends to be more laidback and focused on appreciating the natural surroundings. While you may not find enormous clubs, these establishments offer a friendly setting for a good evening on the islands.

Chapter 7

Practical Tips and Safety Measures

Emergency telephone numbers

For emergencies, dial 110 for fire, 112 for police, and 113 for medical assistance. The emergency hotline centers analyze the situation and arrange the appropriate assistance.

Currency

It's recommended to convert foreign currencies into NOK before your vacation. Many stores in Lofoten don't take EURO or other foreign currencies. Payment cards are extensively used in Norway, and most establishments accept credit cards such as American Express, Diners, Eurocard, Visa, and MasterCard. Foreign debit cards are not generally accepted; we advise you to use an ATM to withdraw Norwegian money instead.

Recovery Services NAF (Norwegian Automobile Federation)

Emergency number in Norway: 08505

Viking Recovery Service Emergency number in Norway: 06000. From overseas - tel.: (+47) 22 08 60 00 Falck Norge. The emergency number in Norway: is 02222.From overseas – tel.: (+47) 33 13 80 80

Driving

Getting penalties in Norway can wreck your trip budget – so be cautious in traffic and stick to these recommendations. Here are some guidelines/laws you must observe while driving in Norway:

Cars must have headlights turned on at all times when driving. The drunk & driving regulations in Norway are stringent. The legal limit is 0.02% blood alcohol concentration.

It is banned to use hand-held phones whilst driving.

Ensure you wear your seatbelt consistently while operating a vehicle.

Follow the speed restrictions, don't drive too fast, and don't drive too slow either.

Tunnels: There are quite a few tunnels here. And there could be people in them! So keep sharp and don't be irresponsible within the tunnels. Some tunnels are also rather narrow, so keep it in mind.

Other things to be careful of: Remember that you share the road with bicycles, people strolling, and animals - even on the major route (E10). Slow down as appropriate and retain your distance as you pass by people and animals.

Parking

The first thing you should do if you want to park anyplace in Lofoten - is to download the "EasyPark" app. Be mindful of the following:

Paying for parking in Lofoten is most widespread in the following municipalities: Vågan, Flakstad, and Moskenes.

Be cautious to look for signage in close vicinity to where you're parked.

Some areas follow various sorts of restrictions than what you may discover in any application.

If you see a sign with a huge "M" on it, it denotes a "meeting place" for automobiles to pass one other. We have these locations on small roadways. It does not have a halt for snapping pictures or parking.

Parking on the side of the road

To free camp in Lofoten is part of the "freedom or right to roam" notion (more about this further down). But parking on the side of the road has several implications:

Motorhomes/campervans should not park too near - if there's a fire, it spreads.

We advise you to consider it again before you park your vehicle for the night. If there's no road (asphalt or gravel), you aren't permitted to drive or park there (part of the motor traffic laws). You may pitch a tent in such regions, but you aren't permitted to park a car and sleep in it if there's no road. In rare circumstances, it may appear like an area is part of some route. But in many such areas, it's due to over-using that space — which should not be utilized for parking in the first place.

There are lots of fantastic campsites in Lofoten – and we suggest staying at any of them on your tour instead.

Electric Cars (EV) and Charging Points

Electric vehicles are becoming more popular and we welcome electric cars on travels around the roads in Lofoten's wonderful surroundings. The development of charging stations increases each passing year and will make it simpler for you to go on a ride. To plan your route in Lofoten, we propose that you download the software "A Better Route Planner", which includes updated maps with charging stations.

Public Transport Bus:

There are capacity limitations of 50% on runs longer than 1,5 hours. If the capacity is filled, a replacement bus will arrive. You purchase tickets in the app "Billett Nordland" shortly before entering the bus because the ticket runs from when you buy it.

Ferry

On the boats, there are automated readings of the automobile signs. You may purchase an "Auto Pass" and then the ticket will immediately be debited from your Auto Pass account. Passengers travel for free.

Express boat: Payment by card and travel pass is available,

Alcohol

You can only purchase wine and spirits at the state-owned "Vinmonopolet" stores, which can be found in most towns. Almost all grocers offer beer, however, please know that officially the sale of alcohol finishes at 8 pm (3 pm on Saturdays, not at all on Sundays). The minimum age is 20 to purchase alcohol, and 18 to buy beer.

Fishing Regulations

Engaging in deep-sea fishing, specifically using a hand line, is complimentary. Note that you are only able to carry 15 kg of filleted fish out of Norway, and you are not allowed to sell your catch.

Lake/River Fishing: For most sites, you need to obtain a license from the owner of the property to fish. But the local license is not valid until you have paid the "fishing fee" from the "Norwegian Environment Agency".. Also, there are rigorous controls for anadromous species, such as Salmon, Sea trout, and Arctic char. Each lake or river has its restrictions that everyone needs to observe.

Clothing

Always be prepared for fluctuations in the weather; it's better to wear too many clothes than too little, so that you may have a fantastic time without worrying about whether you'll be chilly. Summer temperatures might fluctuate between 25°C and 8°C. Check the weather prediction on yr.no and be prepared.

- Summer: Bring a mix of lightweight and warm clothes, and windproof and waterproof outer layers. Good walking shoes/boots can help you make the most of your visit.
- Winter: Wool or thermal underwear, a layer of fleece or wool, and a windproof and waterproof jacket and pants. Don't forget gloves/mittens, a cap, and a scarf. Consider special winter shoes with a wool inner.

Basic Phrases

1. Hello - Hei
2. Good morning - God morgen
3. Good afternoon - God ettermiddag
4. Good evening - God kveld
5. Goodbye - Ha det
6. Yes - Ja
7. No - Nei
8. Please - Vær så snill
9. Thank you - Takk

10. Excuse me / Sorry - Unnskyld

11. Where is...? - Hvor er...?

12. How much is this? - Hvor mye koster dette?

13. Can you assist me? - Kan du hjelpe meg?

14. I don't understand - Jeg forstår ikke

15. I need a cab - Jeg trenger en taxi

16. Menu - Meny

17. Water - Vann

18. Coffee - Kaffe

19. Tea - Te

20. Breakfast - Frokost

21. Lunch - Lunsj

22. Dinner - Middag

23. Cheers! - Skål!

24. One - En

25. Two - To

26. Three - Tre

27. Four - Fire

28. Five - Fem

29. Six - Seks

30. Seven - Syv

Chapter 8

7 Days Itinerary

Day 1: Arrival at Svolvaer

- **Morning**: Arrive at Svolvær, tour the port, and visit the Lofoten War Memorial Museum.
- **Afternoon**: Enjoy a lovely trip to Kabelvåg and visit the Lofoten Aquarium.
- **Evening**: Have supper at Svolvær, tasting local fish.

Day 2: Hiking and Art in Henningsvær

- **Morning**: Drive to Henningsvær. Hike to Festvågtind for spectacular views.
- **Afternoon**: Explore Henningsvær's art galleries, take a leisurely lunch, and meander about the town.
- **Evening**: Dinner at a local restaurant in Henningsvær.

Day 3: Reine and Å Exploration

- **Morning**: Drive to Reine, trek Reinebringen, and visit the hamlet.
- **Afternoon**: Visit Å, tour the Fishing Village Museum, and enjoy a lovely drive across the region.
- **Evening**: Dinner in Reine, appreciating the beautiful surroundings.

Day 4: Nusfjord and Outdoor Adventures

- Morning: Drive to Nusfjord, and tour the UNESCO-listed settlement.
- Afternoon: Enjoy outdoor activities like fishing or kayaking. Take a boat tour to adjacent islands.
- Evening: Seafood meal at a local restaurant in Nusfjord.

Day 5: Beach Day and Relaxation

- Morning: Visit Haukland Beach and Uttakleiv Beach for a relaxed morning.
- Afternoon: Explore neighboring trails or just enjoy the beach. Consider a picnic.
- Evening: Dinner at a local restaurant or a seaside BBQ.

Day 6: Explore Vestvågøy and Viking History

- Morning: Drive to Vestvågøy. Visit the Lofotr Viking Museum and the neighboring Viking settlement.
- Afternoon: Explore the beaches of Unstad and Eggum.
- Evening: Dinner in the picturesque town of Ballstad.

Day 7: Scenic Drive and Departure

- Morning: Take a picturesque drive across the islands, viewing vistas and photographing the sceneries.
- Afternoon: Explore any remaining places of interest or revisit favorite sites.
- Evening: Depart from Lofoten with recollections of its distinctive beauty.

This extended schedule includes a combination of outdoor activities, cultural encounters, and leisure, enabling you to immerse yourself completely in the lovely ambiance of the Lofoten Islands. Adjust the plan depending on your tastes and the weather conditions during your stay.

Conclusion

As part of the process of developing a complete travel guide to Lofoten Island, it is vital to dive into the complexities that make this archipelago a location that is genuinely beautiful. Lofoten, which is located inside the Arctic Circle, is home to a spectacular tapestry of natural beauties, cultural riches, and a multitude of experiences that are sure to leave an indelible mark on the hearts of tourists long after they have left the region.

The breathtaking scenery of Lofoten is the driving force behind the island's popularity. A visual symphony that captures the spirit of untamed beauty is created by the combination of towering peaks, stunning fjords, and completely untouched beaches. From the ethereal brilliance of the Midnight Sun during the summer months to the fascinating dance of the Northern Lights during the winter months, the ever-changing weather produces a dynamic image of the landscape. Every minute spent in Lofoten is like a stroke of the brush on a masterpiece that nature has created.

However, behind the picture-perfect landscapes, Lofoten shows itself to be a living witness to the cultural legacy that has been passed down for several generations. The narrative of a resilient society that is interwoven with the sea is told via the picturesque fishing towns that are embellished with traditional red huts often referred to as rorbuer. The Lofoten Fisheries, which have their origins stretching back to the Viking Age, have had a significant impact on the way of life and customs of the people who live on the island. Visitors have the opportunity to fully immerse themselves in this illustrious past by visiting museums, interacting with people, and taking part in the lively festivals that highlight the distinctive cultural fabric of the area.

Embarking on outdoor activities is a vital component of the Lofoten experience. Hiking routes meander across stunning terrain, affording panoramic views of mountains and seaside panoramas. Kayaking along the crystal-clear seas allows a close interaction with the marine splendor that surrounds the islands. For those wanting a more adrenaline-fueled trip, world-class surfing destinations await on the Atlantic coastline. The opportunities for exploration are as diverse as the environment itself.

Indulging in local food is a sensory trip in Lofoten. From fresh fish direct from the Arctic seas to traditional meals made with passion and competence, every meal is a festival of tastes. Local cafés and restaurants dish up specialties like stockfish, whale steak, and the famed lutefisk, delivering a gastronomic excursion that echoes the variety of the archipelago.

In considering a vacation to Lofoten, one cannot miss the unique sensations given by a Silent Hybrid-Electric Ship Trollfjord Cruise, a three-and-a-half-hour tour of the fjords. This eco-friendly excursion blends the peacefulness of quiet sailing with the majesty of the surroundings, creating a harmonic connection with nature.

In essence, Lofoten Island calls tourists not only as observers but as active players in a tale that transcends time. Whether reveling in the calm of a fishing town, tackling a hard hiking track, or tasting the delicacies of local food, every moment in Lofoten is a chance to connect with the essence of the Arctic. A trip to Lofoten is not just a holiday; it's an immersing expedition into the heart of a pristine Arctic wonderland that leaves an unforgettable impact on those lucky enough to experience its beauty.

Printed in Great Britain
by Amazon

40133128R00079